Praise for

SACRIFICIAL LOVE

With a refreshing and vulnerable admission, the authors invite you into the timeline of their relationship, describing a marital foundation all too familiar for many. Their stories of surrender to the relentless pursuit of a merciful God show that the foundation of the cross is level for every reader, for every marriage. *Sacrificial Love* radiates the transforming message that no amount of brokenness will prevent God's love from redeeming the shattered parts of your story.

Stephanie Broersma,
founder of Reclaimed Ministry, life coach & author of Reclaimed:
Finding Your Identity after Marital Betrayal

While *sacrificial* isn't a word you typically hear in marriage vows, there's no other word that captures the true meaning of a Christ-reflective marriage more fully. If you're wondering if your marriage can withstand your current trials, I pray the testimonies you read here give you the touch of hope you need to fully trust Jesus to breathe a fresh wind into your union. "Now to him who is able to do immeasurably more than all we ask or imagine . . ." (Ephesians 3:20, NIV).

Dr. Jessica McCleese,
licensed clinical psychologist & certified sex therapist

As a couple married for twenty years, we know firsthand how challenging it can be when partners are not on the same spiritual page. *Sacrificial Love*'s heartfelt stories and reflections on the difficulties of being unequally yoked provide deep insight into how these challenges can lead to tension, miscommunication, and compromise. The authors of this book show us that, even in the most trying times, trusting in God's plan can bring about incredible transformation. This is not just a theoretical exploration but a practical and relatable guide, filled with wisdom from the authors' own experiences. *Sacrificial Love* reminds us of the importance of building a marriage on a foundation of shared faith, open hearts, and constant support.

Sacrificial Love is a must-read for anyone looking to strengthen their marriage and faith. It's full of powerful, real-life lessons that we can all learn from—whether you're facing struggles in your relationship or just want to grow closer to each other and to God.

Isiah and Nicole Cater,
leaders of the GraceFilled Marriages Group &
Community at Gateway Church Dallas

Christ's *Sacrificial Love* sets the foundation for selflessness in marriage, but one can only love selflessly if one is his or her whole self. Once I discovered who I was, how God wired me, and how to fulfill my personality needs, I became my whole, authentic self that God created me to be, thus enabling me to show up for my spouse sacrificially and selflessly. Through Christ's love and example, we have learned to love one another with humility and kindness.

Pastor Derwin Ashley,
pastor of Worship/Well Church Groups

Sex, death, and violence. No, it's not the latest murder mystery; it's the book "Sacrificial Love" that you and your spouse need to pick up. If I didn't know some of the couples involved, I would think it was fiction, but it's not. These accounts are real, and if not for the grace of God, this would be a book filled with tragic endings instead of stories of redemption. Every couple should read *Sacrificial Love*.

Robert & Kay Lee Fukui,
co-founders of i61 Inc., business consultants, podcast hosts & authors

Marriage is impossible . . . without God's help! It is the only living metaphor that presents Christ's love for His Bride, the Church, to the world. So, our marriages are more than a relationship; they are a tool God uses to shape us and present Christ to a lost and broken world. *Sacrificial love* will challenge you to draw closer to Christ personally and be more like Christ in your marriage.

Mike Bickley,
lead pastor of Journey Bible Church

Your heart will be inspired by the powerful stories of couples who embraced vulnerability and grew in their faith through difficult trials. Their experiences show how God's divine plan unfolds through both tragedy and triumph. While submitting to God's plan is difficult, these stories illustrate how God is glorified and how the faith of these individuals was strengthened and transformed. One can only be encouraged to think differently about God and draw closer to Him.

Christina Lum,
Jesus follower & ministry leader

But the fruit of the Spirit is love, joy, peace, longsuffering, kindness, goodness, faithfulness, gentleness, self-control (Galatians 5:22–23, NKJV). No one has discussed the fruit of long-suffering until now. *Sacrificial Love* shares stories of resilience and dependence on God in the most trying of times. From the depths of long-suffering to the stories of redemption and restoration, this is a must-read.

Liz Andersen,
founder of Love Remained Ministries & Hope House Coffee

Sacrificial Love is a must-read for couples desiring to break free and embrace God's design for marriage. The ability of the authors to surrender their marriage to God, allowing Him to take ultimate control, is a beautiful reflection of humility and the power of faith in action.

Derrick and Kendra Byrd,
leaders of Marriage and Engagement Life Group at Word Life Church

Sacrificial Love shows how loss and pain can turn into triumph through faith. The vulnerability of the authors highlights God's amazing power and His desire for us to live abundantly, even in suffering.

Mona Hebert,
Jesus follower & ministry leader

SACRIFICIAL LOVE

Husbands and Wives Tell All

F.I.T. in Faith LLC

Virginia Beach, Virginia

Fitinfaithpress.com

Editing: Sharon Miles Frese

Library of Congress Control Number: 2025905427

ISBN: 978-1-7379022-9-4

The moral right of Tamra Andress, as the primary author of this work and founder of F.I.T. Press, has been asserted by her in accordance with the Copyrights, Designs, and Patents Act of 1988.

All rights reserved. Unauthorized duplication is a violation of applicable laws. No part of this publication may be reproduced or transmitted in any form or by any means. Electronic or mechanical, including photocopying, recording, or any information storage and retrieval system, without the express written permission of the publisher (except by a reviewer, who may quote brief passages and/or display brief passages in a short video clip, as part of a professional review).

Unless otherwise noted, scripture quotations are from the (NIV) THE HOLY BIBLE, NEW INTERNATIONAL VERSION®. Copyright© 1973, 1978, 1984, 2011 by Biblica, Inc.™. Used by permission of Zondervan.

Scripture quotations marked (MEV) are taken from THE HOLY BIBLE, MODERN ENGLISH VERSION. Copyright© 2014 by Military Bible Association. Published and distributed by Charisma House.

Scripture quotations marked (NLT) are taken from the Holy Bible, New Living Translation, copyright ©1996, 2004, 2015 by Tyndale House Foundation. Used by permission of Tyndale House Publishers, Carol Stream, Illinois 60188. All rights reserved.

Scripture quotations marked (ESV) are taken from THE HOLY BIBLE, ENGLISH STANDARD VERSION®, Copyright© 2001 by Crossway, a publishing ministry of Good News Publishers. Used by permission.

Scripture quotations marked (NKJV) are taken from the NEW KING JAMES VERSION®. Copyright© 1982 by Thomas Nelson, Inc. Used by permission. All rights reserved.

Scripture quotations marked (AMP) are taken from the AMPLIFIED® BIBLE, Copyright© 1954, 1958, 1962, 1964, 1965, 1987 by the Lockman Foundation Used by Permission. (www.Lockman.org).

Chuck Swindoll's quote originated from *Great Days with the Great Lives*, by Charles R. Swindoll. Copyright © 2005 by Charles R. Swindoll, Inc.

Published by F.I.T. in Faith Press

This Book is Dedicated to . . .

The Lord of Lords and King of Kings.

The One who exemplified Sacrificial Love from the beginning of time.

Our soul's desire is to amplify your name,
boasting in our weaknesses so you may be glorified.

Table of Contents

Foreword By: Dana Che Williams   xv

Introduction By: Tamra Andress

  xxv

Testimony One:	Choosing Love Over Hurt By Joe and Christina Blincoe	3
Testimony Two:	Sifted Through Grief By Dr. Michelle Dickens	15
Testimony Three:	Life Under the Microscope: Being a City Set on a Hill By Dr. Joshua and Randee Steinke	27
Testimony Four:	Unequally Yoked: Breaking Idols and Building Husbands By Jennifer Beeman	39
Testimony Five:	Wounded, Weary, and Worth Fighting For: A Marriage Redemption Story By Steve and Kess Scharff	51
Testimony Six:	A Marriage Built for the Storm By Gary and Tamra Andress	69
Curriculum:	V.I.C.T.O.R.Y. Marriage: A Blueprint for Lasting Love Curriculum for Married Couples By Tamra Andress	85

Acknowledgments   114

Supporting Resources   115

Foreword by Dana Che Williams

INTRODUCTION BY TAMRA ANDRESS

Foreword

By Dana Che Williams

I don't know of another s-word that stops well-intentioned Christians in their tracks like this one.

The word in question is like the many other s-words in the Bible we'd rather pretend aren't there. You know, words such as *submission, surrender,* and *sin*.

We highlight the verses surrounding these words and contextualize them to our liking. But try as we might, they silently linger on the pages of sacred Scripture, bidding our obedience.

Sacrifice.

Just saying it conjures up tortuous images of doubtful and difficult decisions. But deep within our hearts, we know we can't run from the truth: Sacrifice is an essential ingredient for growth.

Cue the *No Pain, No Gain* T-shirts and bumper stickers.

And since I'm on a roll with these hard truths, here's another one: **Love requires sacrifice.**

To ensure we're tracking along the same path, I've defined *sacrifice* as "the act of giving up something of value in exchange for something more valuable or worthy."

Think of a baseball player who bunts the ball in the ninth inning. He knows his opponent's cleat will connect with the bag on first base before he has a chance to, but his teammate will advance to third base and have a greater chance of sliding home and winning the game. That's sacrifice.

Sacrifice sneaks its way into the marriage vows we innocently declare before God and "these witnesses" on what we believe is the best day of our lives. Funny how most weddings take place at an altar . . . the very place of sacrifice. The picture-perfect couple stare deeply into one another's eyes, promising their undying love for richer for poorer, in sickness and in health, forsaking all others until death do they part. Indeed, a lifetime of sacrifice awaits.

I would learn this hard lesson over many years in my marriage as I lay nursing tear-stained pillows and voiceless prayers. *It wasn't supposed to be this way;* I repeated over and over as my mind, riddled with anxiety, looped through scenes of God only knows what went on in those hotel rooms. I thought marriage was a lifelong sleepover with your best friend, just like the blogs said. No one told me grief was often the price of love.

I was only eighteen the morning I vowed to love my husband until my dying day. Three years older than me, Shaun, too, thought this marriage thing would be, for the most part, *easy*. If we truly loved each other, shouldn't it be? Added to our naive notions was the fact that my husband and I had known each other since we were five and eight years old. Our families had long been forged on the foundation of a faithful church. What could possibly go wrong? I shudder as I remember the eighteen-year-old I once was. I didn't get married to sacrifice. I didn't get married to change. I was fine just the way I was, so I thought. I got married to be happy and to make the man I loved happy too. And I failed. So did Shaun. We failed each other multiple times over; we failed our vows, and we failed God. Like most people, the truth was that we were living to make one person happy at all costs—ourselves.

As the weeks turned into months, our love seemed to diminish surprisingly quickly. Simple squabbles turned into serious standoffs. Ordinary offenses grew into unforgivable ugliness. But the worst thing we did was to turn away from one another and pivot outwardly.

I was drowning in a sea of unspoken needs and unmet expectations. It was as if nothing was working. And though I felt invisible to my husband, I felt seen and understood by my male best friend—a guy who I tucked away for safekeeping in case I needed support Shaun couldn't or wouldn't provide. Little did I know that my little contingency plan would be called upon before I had a chance to count the costs. Meanwhile, Shaun got to explore a sense of responsibility-free freedom on his monthly overnight trips for work. Interestingly, he had also been harboring unspoken offenses toward me.

Around the same time, we both took the bait.

Adulterer was not how I would've ever described myself, but that's what I was. Secrecy, silent treatments, and selfish behavior swiftly gave way to sin. My own brokenness shattered my sense of loyalty, integrity, and dignity. But when I found out about my husband's betrayal, it rocked me to my core.

How had we fallen so hard so fast?

We weren't even two years into our marriage, and we had already broken the promise made at the altar—the place of sacrifice.

Fresh out of wishes and willpower, I knew I needed help.

As a child, I had always loved the Lord. I began a vibrant relationship with Him before I hit kindergarten and had felt His presence for as long as I could remember.

How could I have fallen so hard so fast?

The question wouldn't relent. I knew what I needed to do.

My sporadic church attendance increased to nearly every week, and I felt that familiar presence drawing me back in. On a random Wednesday afternoon, sitting in the congregation of a women's conference I felt unworthy to attend, my life turned right side up.

The speaker, a stylish and confident woman, commanded the stage with eyelashes and extensions as long as her preaching. But her words were kind and convicting at the same time. In that moment, it was as if every other woman around me faded into the background, and all I heard was this woman declaring the Word of the Lord to me:

> "But I have this complaint against you. You don't love me or each other as you did at first! *Look how far you have fallen!* Turn back to me and do the works you did at first" (Revelation 2:4–5, NLT, emphasis mine).

And I broke.

I'm not usually prone to public tears, but in that moment, streams of salty surrender slid down my cheeks, washing away the shame and pain I had been carrying for so long. After my affair, I had sense enough to give up my "friend," but I now knew that God hadn't given up on me. I stood to my feet and allowed the love of my faithful Father to realign me to the place I always belonged—in His presence. I rededicated my life to the Lord that day, and I have not looked back.

This is the part of the story where I tell you I went home to find my husband lying prostrate on our living room floor. His Bible lay nearby, stained with tears of torment. He looked up at me and confessed that he, too, had a life-altering encounter with the Lord. I helped him to his feet, and beneath the rays of sunlight peeking through our living room window, we embraced and were instantaneously and instinctively transformed into the husband and wife we were always meant to be.

That is *not* what happened.

Unfortunately, Shaun did not change, and for the next decade, our marriage was ravished by cycles of his infidelity and indecision. My prayers were a mix of complaints, regrets, and demands. I wanted God to be God, but He was taking far too long. It was time for me to take matters into my own hands. I think you know where this is headed. . . .

I would soon learn and relearn that my way of doing things was horribly inadequate. I tried it all: rejection, ultimatums, preaching, begging, and even violence . . . all in the name of the good Lord, of course. But none of it moved Shaun. It just made a bad situation worse.

Dana, do you love me? I heard the Lord ask.

"Why, yes, Lord; you know I love you," I blurted out loud.

Then love him as I have loved you.

If this book were animated, this would be the perfect place to insert the side-eyes emoji. Why was God telling *me* to love my husband when *I* was the one unloved? How was *I* supposed to love a man who was unfaithful to *me*?

Love him as I have loved you.

I didn't want to. He didn't deserve it. Plus, I had the biblical "out" to leave.

Sure, I wanted Shaun to come to love the Lord and honor Him with his whole life, but I didn't want to be the one to show him how it was done. Surely, there was a pastor lying around somewhere that God could use instead of me.

But those seven words would not leave me alone.

Love him as I have loved you.

(For those of you who didn't trust me and counted the words on your fingers, I see you. God is always watching. Insert smiling emoji.)

How on earth could I love a man I didn't even like? I wished I were like all the other good Christian wives I knew who were going through their own struggles in marriage. They seemed to have something I didn't. They could still be nice to their husbands, even when treated unfairly. I wasn't built that way.

But I did love God, and I wanted to please Him with all of my life. So I reluctantly prayed that God would change *me* (thank you, Stormie Omartian). I realized I would need to give up my way of doing things. But that wasn't all. I had to give up my timeline for when I wanted God to "fix my husband."

> *I had to give up control.*

I had to give up self-righteousness.

And I had to give up everything else that stood between me and the altar.

You see, friend, sacrificial love requires you to give up what you're holding onto so tightly. It will require you to place your complete trust in God. It will require you to relinquish all control to the One who holds the stars in His hand.

> "There is no greater love than to lay down one's life for one's friends" (John 15:13, NLT).

> *Jesus paid the ultimate sacrifice for you and me.*

And He had the right to cast us aside because He was perfectly righteous, while we were not. He never sinned. We did. Yet, the apostle Paul gives us a glimpse into the mind and motives of Christ as He broke through galaxies to gain us as heirs of the kingdom.

"Though he was God, he did not think of equality with God as something to cling to. Instead, *he gave up his divine privileges;* . . . he humbled himself in obedience to God and died a criminal's death on a cross. Therefore, God elevated him to the place of highest honor and gave him the name above all other names, that at the name of Jesus, every knee should bow, in heaven and on earth and under the earth, and every tongue declare that Jesus Christ is Lord, to the glory of God the Father" (Philippians 2:6–11, NLT, emphasis mine).

Then, Jesus looks at us and bids us to do the same.

So, how do we enact sacrificial love? We do what Jesus did. In humility, we lay down our self-centered needs and desires (Philippians 2:3–5). When we choose to love in this way, we are reflecting the gospel of Jesus Christ to a world that is lost and longing for lasting love.

Do not attempt this on your own. You will not succeed. However, when you surrender to the Holy Spirit and allow His love to flow in and through you, you will experience a love for the ages. Shaun and I have.

And remember, "For God is working in you, giving you the desire and the power to do what pleases him" (Philippians 2:13, NLT).

God's got the wood and the fire, and He's prepared the altar.

All that's needed now is a sacrifice.

Yours. Mine.

So the world will know.

Dana Che Williams is a speaker, teaching pastor, and podcast host of the Rebuilding US podcast who encourages, equips, and inspires people to step up more confidently and courageously in their lives and relationships.

She is the founder of Thrive Relationships, LLC, and is known for her humor, grace, and candid speaking style. Dana helps churches, ministries, corporations, and individuals tackle communication challenges, implement healthy boundaries, and develop structured rhythms for spiritual and emotional care.

She holds a BA in Communication from Regent University. Dana published her debut novel, The Choice That Changed Her Life, in 2012. She is a regular contributor to christianity.com and has written for numerous other publications. Dana shares her life with Shaun, her handsome husband of twenty-five years, and their fab four: Chris, Cayla, Corey, and Collin in Virginia Beach, Virginia.

Introduction

By Tamra Andress

When topics are dropped into my spirit for these projects, I always sit with the Lord and ask these three questions: *Why now, what for,* and *how*?

Sacrificial love was a persistent phrase I heard in a dark season, one which I'm still currently walking out of, so parts of me thought that perhaps this phrase was just for me. But God wouldn't let it sit in solitude. He told me, "This is my heart," and "Heaviness remains if it's not brought to light." Personally, I was also holding tight to many marriage testimonies that blessed my staying, blessed my capacity, blessed my fight, and blessed my desire for it to be good again because, as Tauren Wells's song sings, "If it's not good, then He's not done."

I positioned this book not to be a premarital guide.

Not to oppose or celebrate divorce.

Not to have one-sided voices of traumatic events.

Not to be hopeful, glossy fairy tales, either.

Instead, I thought of the resilient men and women who have walked through fires— and maybe still are—but are willing and able because of the One who sustains them and calls them blessed. The One who turns impossible situations into possible and probable because they are predestined to showcase His goodness and passion for covenant love. After all, Jesus is the sacrificial love at the core of this concept. Without Him, none of us would have the faith to stick it out or the comfort of knowing we are deeply and richly cared for by a heavenly Father in ways no earthly relationship could ever provide. Without Him, we would not know that the true sacrifice lies in surrendering our wants to our needs and learning to be receivers of His love so that we, too, can be generous givers rooted in forgiveness and peace.

We are fallible humans, most of whom haven't ever fully understood the greatness of the love of God in our own lives. While we may have encounters with Him, it's nearly impossible to grasp "how far and how wide and how deep" His love really is (Ephesians 3:18). And as we get drawn into the sharpening of one another, we realize it can hurt. And, unfortunately, it can be done in our flesh (not well, of course) rather than in our spirit. We make mistakes. We say things we don't mean. We do things we want to do and don't consider the repercussions or outcomes that can greatly affect the nucleus of our once "perfect love," a love that we agreed to and joyously said "I do" to. We get it wrong. But then, when we surrender to His will, He can and will make it right.

> *We get it wrong. But then, when we surrender to His will, He can and will make it right.*

As I mapped out the types of stories I wanted to reveal to the curious, hopeful reader, I didn't have to look very far. Every marriage I know has experienced its fair share of bumps and bruises, and everyone's story is unique. The list below represents the stories of those dear to me, and they all have happy endings, even when the mountains felt impossible to move in the moment. Some of these are included in this book to bless you and give you "hope and a future" (Jeremiah 29:11, NIV).

- A widowed spouse who is now a single mom of a newborn.
- A physically, emotionally, and verbally abused mama of two who was able to break free from manipulation and torment yet still has to co-parent with her perpetrator.
- A military bride who never imagined she'd spend years of her and her children's lives solo parenting, only to welcome home a man experiencing PTSD and seemingly unavailable for deep connection.

- A husband whose wife falls ill unexpectedly, leaving him as both mother and father to their children.
- A couple who has dealt with the torment of losing a child, both in utero and later in life.
- A spouse who has walked through the trenches of the mental health battle of their significant other.
- A seasoned couple with adult children who choose divorce after decades of trying to "make it work for the kids."
- A bride who, despite the appearance of a "happy" marriage, has felt voiceless and alone as her husband chased money and big goals.
- A newly married couple who face the unexpected pressures of sharing space, finances, time, and temperaments they had never noticed or considered before.
- An abandoned wife whose husband had been living a secret life.

The list goes on . . .

While you may be reading this and thinking, "I've never experienced anything quite like this in my life," I know for certain that there are still depths of pain, confusion, loss, hopelessness, and isolation that we all experience, whether individually or collectively. I have also found that grieving can manifest differently in males and females, and these differences can create unexpected tension.

So, after chewing on the concept as a publishing team, we sat secure in Him and His will for this message: to illuminate the chasms that can exist and showcase the bridge building that can happen in and through experiencing His sacrificial love. Because, quite frankly, I don't think anything would flourish without it.

Not shockingly, when we released the idea to the community, there were many marriages that raised their hands to answer the war cry to save, heal, restore, and support the mission of revealing all—not for their own benefit but to glorify Him.

Oddly, though, couple by couple, individual by individual, they started to drop out. There were concerns about the "readiness" of their healing, the reluctance of one spouse to share, the doubt that crept in about their kids' hearts in the long run, or, most commonly, being "just too busy." I call them excuses with pure grace and understanding. But, ultimately, as I took it before the Lord again, questioning if He was sure, if the timing was wrong, or if this was just for me, His peace persisted, and I was certain. It wasn't about how many testifiers there were. It was instead about the boldness of the few, the ones who were willing to open their mouths despite the enemy's tactics to silence; the ones who, no matter what their wholeness or readiness factors were in the flesh, were willing to be like Moses, going forth, even with a stutter.

I've had the gift of officiating several weddings of friends, strangers, and family members. And each time I sit with a couple, asking them about their relationship, their history, their love story, and their wedding day dreams, their innocent passion for "I do" still makes me giddy. Their innocence doesn't denote ignorance, for I'm sure they've borne witness to the challenging marriage scenarios around them. But the thought of that next step, that big yes, that dressed in white, that "You may now kiss the bride" is whimsical and seemingly always one of the happiest days of our lives.

So, I hold space for their love and prepare a message for their future love. Sharing such concepts as the tree of life and the three-stranded cord and perhaps quoting verses from 1 Corinthians on love, I interweave their falling-in-love stories and their words of affirmation for one another, and I anticipate their vows (whether recited or uniquely written). I have an intimate vantage point as we three stand at the altar. I witness the sweet, tender moment as they gaze into each other's eyes, with at least one set filled with tears, to say *I love you* with commitment, sacrificing their individuality for oneness—a shared story moving forward. Not knowing what the future holds, they stand trusting their intuition (regardless of their current relationship with God) that she or he is the one! One of my favorite moments is when I ask them to turn and look at the faces of the family and friends who have gathered to support them. I share with them that these are the people who are meant to remind them of this moment—the pure joy and love they exude today and the vow and commitment they are making to one another "till death do us part." Of the marriages I've overseen, all seven are still intact, but I've seen what can happen when two become one, especially for those without the firm foundation, strength, and pillar that is Christ.

I've been married twice . . . to the same man. We renewed our vows after ten years, some of which were quite tumultuous. And when we said "I do" the second time, it wasn't even remotely the same. Upon reflection, I had no idea what love was the first time I said my vows. I knew of God, but I didn't know Him yet. So I didn't know if this marriage was in His will—I never asked Him. I just went with the butterflies and what made sense, and I loved like I had witnessed and experienced love, which sadly wasn't always pure, righteous, or holy. We navigated all the firsts together, some of which occurred before our marriage, which presented their own unique challenges: our first home, our first big purchase, our first child, and then our second. We rarely fought because we were both "flighters" rather than fighters, running in the opposite direction and eventually sweeping things under the rug to "people please" and keep the peace. It was a seemingly healthy and happy American Dream type of marriage. But four years in and after many prodigal moments in my marriage, I had a radical encounter with Christ in my living room, and everything shifted for me. (You can read more about this event and its specific healing journey in my first best-selling book, *Always Becoming*.)

Ten years later, I now understand what the greatest love of all time, of eternity, did for me, and I know that marriage was so much less about what I could bring to the table for my husband and so much more about how God had designed me to be a wife of noble character. Maturity started to set in. And even through other struggles with our families, finances, and moral failures, God didn't leave us or forsake us, and His great love kept pursuing us.

So round two "I do" was God's idea, or so I thought. In reflection, I recognized my selfishness and eagerness to have the pretty bow on the relationship. I wanted the wedding, just like I did ten years prior after a three-and-a-half-year dating season. I eagerly desired to rewrite that story and relive that "best-day-ever" butterfly experience with the man I loved. This was a much wiser love, a much more rooted love. By this point (fifteen years into our relationship), God had been invited into our marriage in ways we didn't know we needed. We had broken generational curses together. We had fought against powers of darkness and principalities that tried to divide. We had been baptized on both coasts. We had traveled and practiced what I like to call "lights on love." But even still—years later—we face trials that break me.

Why does this happen? Why do we have to experience the rollercoaster that is "love" between man and woman? Why do we choose this relationship even when we'd rather run or hide or quit? We see the unfailing love that sacrificed all and sent His son to die for us on the cross so that we would be in right relationship with Him. No veil. No high priest. Just face-to-face intimacy. In the Word, we read of the bride and the bridegroom exemplified through Christ and His church. We read of promises in our lineage and for our future generations. We say yes to the mandate of the garden: to be, do, have, and multiply. As man and woman were first created, and as we were knit together in our mother's womb, God knew marriage would be a reflection of our relationship with Him. No other union could depict God's love with His people. He secured a contract with Abraham, and from Adam to the second Adam (Jesus), He made good on His promise to restore intimacy with us. We say yes because He said yes to us. We say "I do" because He said I will for eternity. Nothing about it was easy. Can you imagine the torment of watching your one and only son being sent to die for the sake of imperfect humans who can't seem to get it right? I can't. But He could, and He did. And therefore, my yes isn't just to my spouse. It's to the third cord, the union maker, the covenant keeper.

> *We say yes because He said yes to us.*
> *We say "I do" because He said I will for eternity.*

The breaking is meant to rebuild us.

The heartache is meant to lead us to the healer.

The imperfections are meant to be shaped by the perfect one.

The pressure is meant to "pearlize" us.

The pains are meant to prepare us.

But there is likewise the beauty that is marriage.

Sacrifice is also a willingness. It presents the other side of love: the ultimate letting go of self to honor another and the desire to see another live into their abundance and passions. It is to watch someone flourish and be set free in their becoming journey. To be the keeper of someone's deep needs and struggles. To be a resting place of love and a light when the rest of the world feels dark. To be a comforter and a friend, an encourager and a cheerleader, a travel companion and a snuggle partner. It is the wonders of intimacy in purity and trust. A friendship like you've never known in anyone else. An equal nurturer to your legacy. A co-parent to your gifted children. A dream chaser and a play partner for life.

The Father doesn't miss any detail in representing all of who He is in all of who we are as husband and wife: the representation of man and woman, of Adam and Eve, the bride and the bridegroom. And ultimately, every lens of this love is intended to magnify His goodness and mercy that chase us down, even in the darkest valleys. This is what sustains us. This is what strengthens our *yes*, even when faint.

As you dive into these testimonies, may you hold each story with grace and empathy while taking to heart the richness of wisdom that Abba has passed to each of these brave souls. Lean into what He did in the midst of the meanwhile while not comparing or applying any bit of story line to your own journey. The intent is to open you up and then immediately armor you up. No story is greater or less than another. Not one is more traumatic, angelic, purposed, refining, or sanctifying. Ultimately, it's not about us anyway . . . It's about Him.

So here we are, opening the sealed files of our marriage stories—the ones that we hold sacred, the ones that led us to tears, therapy, and, eventually, the feet of Jesus.

Before we dive in, I'd encourage you to pray this prayer with us:

Lord,

I come to you eager for your wisdom and your Word. I come with a heart postured to listen but not to take on any weights of the world. I have a sound mind and ask that you help me in taking every thought captive that may deter me from intimacy with you and my spouse. Jesus, you are my significant other. My significance comes from you. No matter my marital status, you await me with a ring and a robe, always as the comforter and Father and lover that you are. You are my protector, my keeper, and my fortress. I rely on you above everyone and everything else. Seal my heart with your love. Open my eyes to ways I can be refined as a wife/husband, now and forevermore. I surrender my ways to your perfect will, and I request the Holy Spirit to guide me through these chapters and lead me into a deeper knowing of who you are and who I am called to be as a spouse and lover. Abba, mend my broken heart, renew my mind, and allow me to walk more freely into the abundance of promises you have prepared in advance for me and my marriage. I trust you. And I praise you.

Amen.

"Love is patient, love is kind. It does not envy, it does not boast, it is not proud. It does not dishonor others, it is not self-seeking, it is not easily angered, it keeps no record of wrongs. Love does not delight in evil but rejoices with the truth. It always protects, always trusts, always hopes, always perseveres."

1 CORINTHIANS 13:4–7, NIV

Choosing Love Over Hurt

JOE AND CHRISTINA BLINCOE

Testimony One

Choosing Love Over Hurt

By Joe and Christina Blincoe

*I*n our chapter, Christina and I will explore how the journey of marriage constantly calls us to lay down personal desires for a love that serves the other. Through the unexpected challenges and stretching seasons, we will examine how surrendering control and seeking God's guidance have transformed our marriage and our understanding of unconditional love. This chapter is an invitation to embrace a love that draws us closer to Christ as we grow closer to each other.

Before we dive into this subject, it is important to understand what it means to love and be loved. *Love* is a word that has lost much of its meaning over the last few decades, but the definition of love provided in 1 Corinthians 13 is clear on how we are to love.

Joe's Voice:

Having grown up in a Christian home with parents who have been together since middle school, I have a deep respect for marriage and commitment. Five years into my own marriage, however, I found that my spouse's idea of commitment was very different, and she asked for a divorce. This left me questioning whether there was such a thing as real and lasting love. How could I ever trust again, fully give my heart to someone, or risk being hurt?

I was definitely not looking for a relationship when I met Christina; she completely caught me off guard. After getting to know her for a while and hearing her story, I realized she wasn't one to give up easily; she was a fighter. Despite being deeply hurt during her childhood and in her marriage, she was fully devoted to her kids and her vows. For years, she had sacrificed, trying to make a relationship work that had been sabotaged early on. When we finally said our "I dos," I knew I had met the love of my life, the one I would be with for the rest of our lives.

For me, love is so much more than respect or admiration; it's far beyond the physical attraction that often catches us up in the initial stages of courtship. It boils down to one thing for me, and that is ultimately the subject that the authors in this book are focused on: the idea of "sacrificial" love. I have heard so many people say things like "I would never give a person that kind of power over me," or "Why would I open myself up to be hurt like that?" It is ideas like this that cripple so many relationships; it's what sours the concept of love for so many couples. To truly experience love, you must be open to the possibility of hurt. If you are holding anything back for yourself, you are not truly loving anyone, and, ultimately, you are hijacking your own happiness. Understand that we do not say this lightly, as we have gone through some pretty painful moments in our individual pasts.

It is important to get to the root of the struggles, pain, and associated scars your spouse has in their life. This is where the most significant work of love and understanding needs to happen. In the popular book *The Five Love Languages*, Gary Chapman talks about the importance of knowing your spouse's love language. And while this is super important, it is equally important to know what truly hurts your spouse or triggers negative responses in them. For instance, my wife and I have experienced relationships that left us scarred in terms of trust. Because of this, we tend to question things more than the average person. In Christina's case, there was infidelity on the part of her spouse that left her always questioning if I was really working late, really going to a men's group, or really in love with her. In my case, I experienced feelings of inadequacy and doubt, making it difficult to truly trust someone when they said, "I love you."

When we study, learn, and apply how God loves us, it reduces the pressure considerably. Feeling loved by our Father makes it easier to cope with times when we don't feel loved by our partner. But this doesn't give us a pass. We need to make sure we are intentional in how we show each other love. If we are both secure in our relationship with God, through His example, we will truly understand what love looks like—pure, unconditional, and grace-filled love.

If we are secure in our relationship with God and trust in our partner's relationship with Him and their love for us, then the situations that might typically cause us pain or make us question our worth will hold less power. We can find peace in knowing that our Father's love surpasses all. Every relationship will have misunderstandings and moments when words are spoken in haste but not truly meant. In those times, it's easy to feel as though we have lost our place of importance with our partner. However, as Christians, we must remember that our standing in God's eyes remains unshaken. Unfortunately, these vulnerable moments in our relationships create openings for the enemy to plant seeds of doubt, insecurity, and resentment. These lies surround us daily, constantly pressing in, and it's all too easy to believe them—especially when they seem to come from those we love most.

Truth is the only thing that can combat these lies. The Bible is our source for the truth; just the fact that it exists is a testament to the love the Father has for us. Consider for a moment how impossible it should be for text written on papyrus or linen to survive the ages, be translated and copied into every language, and still be as relevant to us today as it was when it was written. That same Bible begins with God creating man in His image.

Can you imagine that God, who has the power to create all the beauty this world holds, created us in His image? To some extent, every book in the Bible speaks of God's love for us, but it is our nature to make things hard on ourselves. We always fall short, but God loves us so much that He sent Jesus, His son, to live a perfect life in order to show us how it's done. Jesus's life is the perfect example of sacrificial love. He knowingly laid His life down to cover our sins and shortcomings. Jesus bridges the gaps in our own ability to forgive and shows us, with His help, that nothing is too big for us to overcome, not even death.

> *Jesus bridges the gaps in our own ability to forgive and shows us, with His help, that nothing is too big for us to overcome, not even death.*

When Christina and I first got married, my "I do" was rooted in love and commitment, but it was also shaped by my own understanding and emotional limitations. Over time, I've learned not to take situations or words as personal attacks but to recognize there is often a deeper issue or fear behind the emotion. As a couple, we've discovered the importance of unpacking these underlying concerns together and learning how to pivot or approach each other with compassion and understanding.

Sometimes, that means giving Christina the space she needs; other times, it means leaning in and being present. My "I do" today is even deeper and more mature, anchored in a faith that has grown stronger through the challenges and victories we've shared.

Christina's Voice:

Childhood plays a significant role in shaping our understanding of marriage and how we approach it. Growing up without a healthy example of marriage left me deeply determined at the age of twenty to make my own marriage succeed. I clung tightly to my commitment, driven by the belief that divorce was unbiblical. However, this mindset created emotional and spiritual bondage as I wrestled to align my painful experiences with my faith.

For years, I didn't fully understand that there are situations where divorce is both justified and biblical, particularly in cases of unfaithfulness when one partner remains unrepentant and unwilling to change. My refusal to consider this reality stemmed from fear and a misunderstanding of God's heart for marriage. It wasn't until I sought help through marriage counseling and received guidance from trusted elders and pastors in my church that I began to see things differently.

Through prayer and their wisdom, I realized what I was enduring in my marriage was far from God's design. I learned that God's desire for marriage includes restoration and freedom. While His plan is always for reconciliation when possible, there are times when separation is necessary to protect and honor the dignity of His children. In this journey, I discovered the beauty of God's redemptive love and His ability to bring healing, even when difficult decisions must be made.

At the start of our marriage, Joe and I faced many challenges. Both of us carried past wounds into our relationship, and we had to navigate these while raising a family. Joe had never been a father, so he had to learn the patience and intentionality required to guide and teach our young boys. At the same time, I had to learn to surrender my expectations and embrace God's plan for our family.

God used this season to teach me the importance of letting go of control. He led me to share this journey in a chapter titled "Need for Control" in *The Joy-Full Entrepreneur: Awaken, Renew, Transform*, an Amazon best seller. In this chapter, I reflect on how surrendering my need for control allowed me to entrust my life and business to God. As a believer, I hold fast to the truth that though we make choices that shape our lives, the ultimate control belongs to God. When we align ourselves with His will, He leads us to a life of peace, purpose, and freedom in Christ.

I was thirty-three when I met Joe, my amazing husband of seventeen years. Our paths crossed through our church, and I soon learned that he had experienced the deep pain of divorce. Though he didn't have children from his previous marriage, the wounds he carried from that relationship ran deep. We agreed to take things slowly, choosing to build a friendship rooted in trust and shared faith. I wasn't ready to date, but I cherished our long talks and the way our conversations drew us closer to God.

During this time, Joe and I began serving as volunteers, helping children who were navigating the pain of divorce, just as my two young boys were. God used this season to bring profound healing to all of us. One Christmas, we decided to forgo our own celebrations to provide for a young family in need. Two children in our class, who were being raised by their single father, had nothing for Christmas. That year remains one of my most treasured memories. We shopped for groceries, toys, and bikes for the family, embracing the joy of giving without expecting anything in return.

Later, after Joe and I got married, we faced a season of uncertainty when Joe lost his job. Yet, God's faithfulness shined brightly. One day, we found gifts left on our front porch, a tangible reminder of His provision through our church family. These moments revealed God's loving care and reassured us that no circumstance is beyond His power.

Joe's love for my boys reflected God's heart for adoption and fatherhood. He adopted them as his own, desiring that they grow up knowing the unwavering love of a father. To this day, we celebrate the day of their adoption as "Gotcha Day," a beautiful reminder of God's redemptive work in our family.

Although we faced challenges trying to have a child together, God used that time to strengthen our faith. In His perfect timing, He blessed us with a son, Isaac, whose name means "laughter"—a fitting reminder of the joy and humor God weaves into the details of our lives. That moment was a testament to God's faithfulness and perfect timing when we trust in Him. God has been our anchor through every joy and trial, showing us that His plans are far greater than we could ever imagine. Our story is one of His redemption, provision, and steadfast love.

TobyMac's beloved song "Made to Love" is a beautiful reminder that we were created to love and be loved by God. He will never leave us, and our hearts are called to surrender everything to Him. This song climbed the charts in 2007, the same year Joe and I were married, making it even more special to us. Over the years, we've cherished the sweet memories of taking each of our boys to a TobyMac concert, planting seeds of faith in their hearts, and reminding them God is always with them, patiently waiting and never letting go.

Looking back, I see how my understanding of marriage has grown since I said "I do" to Joe. When we first got married, my commitment was grounded in love and hope, but over the years, my "I do" has deepened into a covenant shaped by God's transforming work in my life. Through prayer, Scripture, and seeking God's guidance, I've experienced healing inside and out, becoming a better partner and mother.

To read more about this transformative journey, check out my chapter titled "Living in the Truth of His Love" in the book *Before She Knew Jesus*. In the chapter, I share how I moved from merely knowing about Jesus to experiencing the profound reality of being fully known and loved by Him.

Diving into Our Struggles as a Couple

Joe and I have faced challenges in our marriage, particularly in three key areas: trust, financial self-control, and making decisions on raising our children to be self-sufficient. These struggles have shaped our journey and revealed areas where God is still refining us. Let's take a closer look at each.

1. Trust and Inadequacy

At the heart of our struggles with trust is fear—fear of not being enough and fear of losing each other if we fall short. Both Joe and I long to be truly seen, heard, and known. For Joe, this often means questioning his worth—whether he is enough in my love, whether he can provide for our family, and what defines his identity. When he feels unheard or inadequate, it holds him back from pursuing new opportunities, leaving us both feeling stuck.

For me, the fear of losing control often drives my actions. The fear of losing my job and not providing enough for our family, combined with the pressure to maintain perfection, keep me trapped in a cycle of feeling like I have to carry everything on my own. I've often told myself I'm all alone, but the truth is Joe is there—faithfully showing his love in tangible ways. Whether it's fixing something in the house, making sure I have gas in the car, or caring for the kids, Joe's actions reflect a steady presence I sometimes overlook in my own striving.

Through prayer and seeking God's truth, we're learning to surrender these fears to Him. Scripture reminds us: "Do not conform to the pattern of this world, but be transformed by the renewing of your mind" (Romans 12:2, NIV). Trust grows when we root ourselves in God's perfect love, knowing our worth and identity are secure in Christ, not in our performance or what we provide for ourselves.

> *Trust grows when we root ourselves in God's perfect love, knowing our worth and identity are secure in Christ, not in our performance or what we provide for ourselves.*

2. Self-Control with Finances

Joe and I have jobs that provide well for our family, yet we often find ourselves living above our means. In our desire to compensate for the ways we feel we've fallen short as parents, we tend to spend too much on our family, children, and lifestyle. This pattern stems from wanting to heal past hurts, but it has led us away from practicing good stewardship.

God has entrusted us with resources, and we're learning to honor Him by discerning His timing and priorities for how we use them. Are we stewarding the gifts He has given us well? Are we tithing and returning to Him what is already His? Proverbs 3:9–10 (NIV) reminds us to "Honor the Lord with your wealth, with the firstfruits of all your crops; then your barns will be filled to overflowing, and your vats will brim over with new wine." True financial freedom comes from aligning our hearts with God's purpose and trusting in His provision.

3. Teaching Our Children Independence

One of my greatest struggles has been letting go of our adult children so they can learn independence. Joe and I have modeled a strong work ethic, yet we continue to step in to help them, even when it's no longer necessary. While our desire to leave a legacy for our children drives much of what we do, we have had to ask ourselves: *Am I sacrificing my own joy, happiness, and marriage in the process?*

Scripture calls us to raise children in the way they should go (Proverbs 22:6) and to trust God with their future. Leaving a legacy isn't just providing financial stability; it's modeling faith, resilience, and trust in God. By holding on too tightly, we have come to realize we may be hindering their ability to grow into the independent adults God has called them to be.

These challenges are a work in progress, but through God's grace, we are learning and growing. As we submit our fears, finances, and family to Him, we trust He will continue to refine us and guide us into the abundant life He has planned.

The word *love* appears in the Bible over 500 times in various translations, and *fear* is mentioned more than 350 times. God highlights the relationship between these two words in 1 John 4:18 (NIV): "There is no fear in love. But perfect love drives out fear." This verse reminds us that when we fully experience God's love, it eliminates fear. True love and fear cannot coexist because God's perfect nature provides security and peace. His Word is not only powerful but also precious, inviting us to trust Him fully.

> *1 John 4:18 (NIV): "There is no fear in love. But perfect love drives out fear."*

So, how do we overcome these areas of struggle in our relationship? Here are three steps grounded in faith:

Step 1: Full Surrender to God

The first step is to give your struggles over to God in complete surrender. Pray and ask Him to reveal the root of these challenges and limiting beliefs. Seek His guidance to replace these patterns with His truth and a healthier way of living. As a couple, pray together about these areas of struggle, keeping the lines of communication open. Recognize that once the children are grown and out of the home, God calls you back to one another. Cultivate a relationship that honors, loves, and desires your spouse as the partner God has given you.

Step 2: Clear Communication with Your Family

Communicate with your family about the changes you are making to align your life and marriage with Christ. Let them know your priorities are rooted in God's design: Christ first, followed by your marriage, and then your children and grandchildren. As you make these adjustments, lean into God's wisdom and grace, trusting that these realignments will bring lasting peace and joy to your family.

Step 3: Surround Yourself with a Faith-Based Community

Accountability and support are essential. Surround yourselves with a community of believers who can encourage and challenge you in your walk with Christ. For Joe and me, this has included life groups at our church, where we connect with other families raising children of similar ages, Bible studies tailored for men and women, and faith-based business leadership groups. Doing life together with others who share your values provides strength and encouragement as you navigate the challenges of marriage and family.

Think about times when your focus was on the past or when your mind was consumed by hurt. In Revelation 21:4 (NIV), God reminds us that "He will wipe every tear from their eyes. There will be no more death' or mourning or crying or pain, for the old order of things has passed away." When we embrace this truth in our relationships, we experience healing, joy, and freedom.

God's design for relationships calls us to love sacrificially, trust Him completely, and walk in faith, knowing that His perfect love casts out fear. By surrendering to Him, communicating with one another, and building a supportive community, we can experience the fullness of His blessings in our marriages and families.

When you choose love over hurt, you reflect God's nature and His ability to transform brokenness into healing and redemption. It's not an easy path, but it's one that brings peace, growth, and a deeper connection with God and those you love. As we are reminded in Romans 8:28 (NIV), choosing love is a decision to trust in God's power to restore: "And we know that in all things God works for the good of those who love him, who have been called according to his purpose."

Choosing Love Over Hurt
JOE AND CHRISTINA BLINCOE

How can we boldly pray together for the things we need to hand over to God?

As a couple, how can we lean into God's Word in order to trust Him in every area of our lives, especially when we feel weak and tired?

How can we speak life into our relationship and show more intentional love so the other feels valued and finds comfort?

Christina is a Christian business leader, motivational speaker, and number-one Amazon best-selling author. She is known for inspiring audiences with her powerful journey of transformation, her passion for business, and her expertise in teaching others how to run profitable, debt-free, side-hustle businesses while having Joy! Through her speaking and mentoring, she empowers individuals to align their values with their work, creating both impact and financial freedom. She is a co-author in The Joy-Full Entrepreneur: Awaken, Renew, Transform, released in November 2024, and the devotional Before She Knew Jesus, released in January 2025.

Joe is the entrepreneur behind Sweet Streams Lavender, a thriving lavender farm and online boutique business, where he combines his entrepreneurial skills with his faith-driven purpose. Joe is an industrial designer by trade and is on staff as lead facilities manager of their church. He has dedicated over twenty-four years to serving in various volunteer and leadership roles in the church family.

Joe and Christina started Sweet Streams Lavender in 2015, focusing on each other's strengths to maximize their time and make the most intentional connections with their community. Their mission is grounded in faith, values, and love for family, friends, partners, and customers they call friends. Joe and Christina are here to help others find beauty in themselves.

"Simon, Simon! Indeed, Satan has asked for you, that he may sift you as wheat. But I have prayed for you, that your faith should not fail; and when you have returned to Me, strengthen your brethren."

LUKE 22:31–32, NKJV

Sifted Through Grief

DR. MICHELLE DICKENS

Testimony Two

Sifted Through Grief

By Dr. Michelle Dickens

I can still feel the coldness of the steel table on my back as I lay there, looking up at the monitor to see if the dye being pushed through my fallopian tubes would flow freely without any blockage. Preston and I had been married for over two years and, like any other couple, wanted to start a family. I knew it would be challenging, as I have had irregular monthly cycles since my teenage years. Several years before we met and married, I had laparoscopic surgery and began cycling regularly. I thought it would be a little easier to become pregnant, but none of that would end up being the problem. As I looked at the monitor above my head in the corner of the room, I saw the dye come to a dead stop halfway through. The technician must have thought that pushing the liquid through with more pressure might help, but I felt it, and it nearly lifted me off the table. "*STOP!*" I shouted. He did, and at that moment, my dreams of having children crashed in on me. I remember my immediate thoughts: *It's your fault. You're the reason you can't have children. I guess that's better than it being Preston's fault.*

Satan found a way into my head. I believed I wasn't complete unless I could bear children and feared being looked down upon by others, especially mothers. Our identities can be wrapped up in something or someone if they are not anchored in God. Think about how we often greet one another. Men will initiate conversations by asking, "What do you do for a living?" while women will ask, "How many children do you have?" I had no desire to deal with that question, nor did I want to figure out how I would respond. Depending on the day and my mood, especially during those immediate years, I would answer that our children were in heaven or that we had none. With the realness of not being able to give birth to our own children, all I knew to do was take my heart to God and cry—until I didn't anymore.

Preston was on active duty in the US Air Force when we married, with only five years remaining before he retired after serving twenty-one years. He went on a couple of short-term deployments, and during his second deployment, God taught me one of the first hard lessons I would learn during my marriage: I leaned on my husband's power and strength more than I leaned on God's. I loved God with all my heart, but as a new wife, I had unconsciously let Preston slip onto the throne of my heart, giving him responsibilities over my well-being that did not belong to him. I learned years later that the source, the origin of my identity, love, completeness, and well-being, had to begin in Christ alone. After Preston returned from this second deployment, I began to feel unwell. I didn't have a cold or flu-like symptoms; I was just feeling . . . off. Well, that was because I didn't know what it felt like to be pregnant—but my doctor confirmed I was nine weeks along! At that moment, I realized that what man says *can* be true, but what God has in store for us *is* TRUTH! We were overjoyed, stunned, and elated! Until . . .

> *I learned years later that the source, the origin of my identity, love, completeness, and well-being, had to begin in Christ alone.*

When I was nineteen weeks pregnant, I began experiencing a more intense pain than I had felt in previous weeks. Nurses and doctors told me it was normal because my body was "stretching," and it was a part of being pregnant. One day, shortly after that experience, I was sitting at my desk at work and felt like I was bleeding. Thankfully, or so I thought, there was only a clear fluid. When I called the nurse to tell her what was happening, she told me to come to the hospital. I arrived and breathed a sigh of relief when I saw our baby's heartbeat on the ultrasound monitor, but then the doctor came in . . . "I am sorry to tell you that you are four centimeters dilated," she said. I just stared at her because I had no idea what she was talking about since this was my first child. When she saw I wasn't getting it, she said, almost in a whisper, "You're losing your baby." The doctor told me to call Preston at work and tell him to get there quickly. When I called, he sounded just as confused as I was; I just saw our baby's heartbeat, and other than the back pain, I was feeling fine.

Preston arrived, and as the doctor explained everything to him, I lay there on the table, staring at our child and resisting what the doctor was saying. Our baby girl was fully developed to the point she was supposed to be, with a strong heartbeat. *Surely, the doctor didn't know what was going on.* It's amazing how our minds create their own narrative when we are in crisis or denial. I convinced myself the doctor had no idea what she was talking about, so I told her, "Just check me into the hospital. I will lie in bed until it's time to give birth. That's all." The doctor asked to speak to Preston outside the room. I lay there, planning to tell him what to bring for my hospital stay. When he came back, I sat up on the edge of the table, and he sat in a chair in front of me. My husband calmly took my hands and looked into my eyes. "I need you to let them take the baby," he said. "If you don't, I could lose both of you."

Friends, at that moment, as I gazed above my husband's head, trying to absorb what he was saying, I believe that I caught a glimpse of Christ, with His nail-pierced hands, whispering to my heart, "You're saying yes to *Me*. Listen to your husband and say yes to *Me*. Trust *Me*." I looked back at him, our eyes filling with tears, and whispered, *okay*. In that moment, I experienced precisely what Paul meant when he wrote, "Wives, submit to your own husbands, *as to the Lord*" (Ephesians 5:22, ESV, emphasis mine). As wives, God shows us in this verse how we are ultimately submitting to *Him* through our husbands and trusting *Him* with outcomes. Please hear me. I am not talking about abusive or, unrepentant, sinful situations. If that is your story, remove yourself as quickly as possible. But in this situation, God showed me what submission in love could look like and the kind of peace that comes with it.

In April 2002, Alexis was born at nineteen weeks. There was a lot going on that day, but one thing I remember clearly: God was tangibly present through other believing friends, our pastor, and even some of the nurses. As a result of their love and care, we experienced the peace that surpasses all understanding (Philippians 4:7). I thought Preston and I would be okay, and what's more, we had found out I *could* get pregnant when the doctors said I *couldn't*. We could try again. . .

Because I gave birth to our first child in the second trimester, I was considered high risk when I became pregnant a second time, and I got to see our baby's heartbeat often. Everything was going well—until it wasn't. Around the fifteenth week of pregnancy, Preston and I returned home from running errands and sat down to eat dinner. Once again, I felt like I was bleeding, but this time, I was. We went to the emergency room, and when our doctor came in, I could tell by her face what she was about to say: "You are two centimeters dilated, and we need to deliver your baby." Something deep inside me broke completely in half—it was my heart. I went completely numb and said with no emotion, "I've done this before, so let's get this over with."

At that moment, everything went black. In that moment, I learned what it feels like to have the very foundation beneath you collapse. I felt like I was spiraling into a deep black hole with no bottom, and I didn't care. In hindsight, I let go. I let go of God. I let go of hope. I let go and sank into a darkness I didn't know existed. This was the beginning of my depression, a condition I didn't realize I was experiencing until several years later. After all, *Christians aren't supposed to be depressed* (big eye roll here)! Joshua, our second child, was born at fifteen weeks in October 2003.

Preston and I went back to going through the motions. I moved my body parts to do whatever the next thing was. Seven months later, I was pregnant again. I wasn't excited, nervous, or sad; I felt nothing and wasn't sure I cared. We had the same doctor, and she concluded I had an incompetent cervix and strongly recommended I go on bed rest at twelve weeks. That was hard. Preston and I worked full-time, which meant one full income was going away, and my husband would have to do everything himself. I was more worried about how he felt than I was about having the baby. But let me tell you, although I could see it was a rough time for him, he walked through that season with as much compassion, dignity, strength, and kindness as he possibly could, and I am forever grateful.

By the time we got to twelve weeks, I started to let my heart attach just a little bit to the idea of having this baby. I thought that with my cervix sewed shut and being on bed rest, we might make it to the end and finally have a baby to take home. We didn't. When I was twenty-one weeks, the longest I had carried a child, I began to feel the same type of back pain I experienced with our first baby girl, and the doctor admitted me into the hospital for full bed rest. One week later, at twenty-two weeks, my water broke, and I delivered our third child, Bryanna, into the arms of Jesus. I was done, done with trying to have a child, done with thoughts about adopting a child . . . just done. We had delivered all three of our children—Alexis at nineteen weeks in 2002, Joshua at fifteen weeks in 2003, and Bryanna at twenty-two weeks in 2004—into the arms of Jesus.

I want to take a moment to share some of my husband's experiences and emotions through all of this, especially after our third child. Joshua, our second child, was the one that broke me, but it was Bryanna, our third child, that broke my husband. A friend shared with me Preston's experience as he was overcome with grief and anger while in the waiting room. When the doctor came out to tell him how I was doing, my husband rose up and directly questioned her. "Why? Why does this keep happening? You said this would work!" He was angry, hurt, and probably exhausted from carrying the weight of it all. My friend said it was the most beautiful, intense moment she had ever seen, and the doctor was kind, gentle, and understanding. The loss of all three children had taken its toll.

The extensive details of what I call our "journey through hell" are for another time, but the impact grief had on us was crushing. More than two decades after losing our children, I learned that grief and marriage are two of the sharpest tools God uses to reveal what is inside of us. God never shows us our sin so that we can use it as a bat to beat ourselves with; He shows us our sin so we can "Come boldly to the throne of our gracious God. [Where] we will receive his mercy, and we will find grace to help us when we need it most" (Hebrew 4:16, NLT).

Pain and suffering are no respecters of persons and give us no strength to hold up masks. This duo drains us of strength and tears down walls, exposing our true selves. But oh, my friend, when we are weak, our God is strong (2 Corinthians 12:10). Preston and I were simply living in a hard space and taking out our hurt feelings and bad emotions on one another, along with everything else we brought into the marriage from our childhoods. As a professional counselor, I have gained a better understanding of how the things that occur in our lives from the very beginning shape our thoughts and behaviors, but until we do some work (whether in therapy or with a mature and trusted friend we permit to speak truth over us), we will remain a shallow shadow version of ourselves rather than the powerful expression of the light and love of Christ!

As Preston and I traversed the halls of hell for the next several years, there was a time when I wanted out of the marriage. I wanted it to all be done, and I wanted the arguing and hurt to stop. I asked if he would go to counseling with me, but he said we could figure it out.

No, we couldn't. We had tried for the past twelve to thirteen years.

On one July 4th, after yet another argument, we went to watch fireworks. As I stood on the bed of his truck, watching the display from a distance, he said, "We might as well get a divorce." Without pause, I told him, "You get the papers, and I promise I will sign them." I wasn't going to take the first step, but at that moment, I was willing to follow.

I am so thankful he didn't get the papers.

I went to counseling by myself, thinking it would help me heal and learn how to live in a space with someone I couldn't get along with. After a couple of sessions, the counselor asked me to ask Preston to come see him. I told him he wouldn't and that I had given up in my mind that he would ever come. He responded, "This time, don't make it about him. Ask if he will come to see me so I can help YOU." Wait! What? I wasn't the problem (another big eye roll)! I laughed out loud typing that because it is what so many of us believe. With all our hearts, we think or say, "If only my spouse would get it together, we could be fine." If you have said that to yourself, I want to let you in on a little secret: You are part of the problem, and, possibly, you may be the whole problem. I realized much later that I was definitely part of the problem and, depending on the day, I took the lead role.

Preston eventually went to see the counselor, and after a couple more times on his own, our counselor brought us in together. I was nervous, but for the first time in years, I also had a little bit of hope. We would have several more years and miles ahead of us to heal and grow, first as individuals in Christ and then together. On this side of it all, however, I can honestly say I would do it all over again because of all I gained in Christ. When we lost Alexis, Jesus gave me His peace, which simply makes no sense. When we lost Joshua, Jesus held me in the grip of His power as I traversed the steep, dark hallways of grief and depression. When we lost Bryanna, Jesus gave me a glimpse of His glory that continues to this day. When I lost the marriage I imagined, God resurrected a love and joy in our marriage that far surpasses all I could ever ask or imagine.

At the end of the day, Preston and I were simply not communicating in a healthy way. He wanted his way, and I wanted mine. We were both right but failed to realize we were also both wrong. I remember a mentor telling me once, "One of you will have to die," meaning, as Paul wrote in Galatians 5:24 (NLT), one of us needed to be willing to nail "the passions and desires of [our] sinful nature to [the] cross and [crucify] them there." At that moment, all I could think about were the many ways *he* needed to die. In one of my morning times with Jesus, I heard a faint, gentle whisper in my heart: "Why is my love not enough? You are the apple of *My* eye; why is that not enough?" That crushed me. I loved Jesus with all my heart, or so I thought, but I had let my husband sneak onto the throne of my heart in place of Jesus. God showed me later how He was calling both Preston and me to Himself, and if only one of us responded, He would and could work through one of us for both of us.

Grief is messy, chaotic, and uncontrollable. It is often the first time humans encounter the reality that this earth is not our home, and the control we presume to have, we learn we never had. Grief overcomes you and can grip you in ways that become your identity . . . if you let it. There is a significant distinction between the one who says, *I will grieve forever* and the one who says, *I am wrestling with grief in this season, but I know joy will come in the morning!* The morning may not come the next day, the next week, or even in the next month or year. Morning comes when it comes, but it does come. Please hear my heart; I have a deep relationship with grief and all its extended family members: depression, anger, anxiety, and so on. If you are new on the grief journey, please take the time you need to heal. Grief is real, and all the things that stem from it take hold, tossing and sifting us violently to and fro in this world. But we do not have to let it toss us around forever. While the journey may be long, it is not permanent . . . unless we choose for it to be. No one wants to be in pain, but for some reason, we often mesh our pain from grief with our loved ones and won't let go. I encourage my clients to release their loved ones (or whatever they are holding onto) to Jesus. Our Savior doesn't ask us to let go; He asks us to trust Him.

While Preston and I do not have children on this side of heaven, along with our other losses and various trials, I can testify that grief has transformed the way I view people and this world, but it does not define who I am. Jesus doesn't halfway heal because He didn't halfway die. Just as I am not halfway saved, I can choose not to be halfway healed. Half a healing leads me to cling to and glorify my loved ones or the traumatic experiences I walked through instead of seeking a deeper, right-now healing that glorifies God *because* of the grief and crises I experience. When people ask if we have children, I use the opportunity to speak of the right-now healing Christ has given me. I share about the divine exchange that occurred with the loss of Alexis, Joshua, and Bryanna when Jesus gave me His peace, His power, and His glory. It strengthens our faith to remember who God is, recall what He has done, and rest in Him.

My "I do" when we stood at the altar twenty-seven years ago involved my own expectations of what a husband should do to fulfill my every need and complete me. My "I do" involved a knight in shining armor who would be strong for both of us. My "I do" said we would pray together every day, serve and worship the Lord together in perfect harmony, and love one another perfectly. My "I do" was rooted in what I thought I needed, what would make me happy, and what my husband could do and be for *me*. Now, my "I do" stands on the promises of Christ alone. My "I do" grounds all my expectations in Christ because *He* is my first husband. My "I do" revels in the extra love and spice I get from my king because, as he puts it, his "I do" stands on the Sovereignty, Salvation, and Sanctification of Jesus Christ through the power of the Holy Spirit. We went from being fully dependent on one another for happiness to being fully God-dependent for a deeper joy. Jesus is THE strand that holds us together, and without Him, we are not.

> *We went from being fully dependent on one another for happiness to being fully God-dependent for a deeper joy.*

After Joshua was born, the Lord led me to Luke 22:31–32, where He told Peter about Satan asking to sift him as wheat and how He prayed for his *faith*. Do you see it? It is our *faith* Jesus prays for while we are here on this earth, not our wants or our selfish desires for money, riches, or success. He does not pray for us to have a healthy marriage, a house full of kids, or for our loved ones to live forever until He returns. Instead, He prays for our *faith* because it is our *faith in Him* that carries us through every trial we encounter. It is our *faith* in Him that strengthens us when we are weak. It is our *faith* in Him that comforts us, heals us, and makes us whole again in His time and in His way. We are on a faith journey, my friends. Jesus knows the way and prays that our *faith* won't fail us. Focus on Jesus, not the journey.

Sifted Through Grief
DR. MICHELLE DICKENS

Whether you are in the middle of a crisis or can see light at the end of the tunnel, pause for just a moment, take a deep breath, and ask yourself what is one kind gesture you could extend to your spouse. *Then, think of one kind gesture you would like to receive.*

If you are at the beginning or in the middle of your healing journey, *what is one small step you can take to draw near to Jesus, your Healer* (i.e., find one thing to be grateful for at the end of each day; read one Bible verse for the day, etc.)?

If you are on the other side of your grief journey, in *what way has God specifically strengthened your* faith, and how can you comfort someone in need with the comfort you received from Christ Jesus?

Prayerfully Reflect
Take the time to prayerfully reflect with the Lord on where you are in your grief journey and how he is working with you in the midst.

Michelle is passionate about seeing people connect with Jesus, helping them cultivate a genuine faith that has a genuine impact on where they live, work, and play. As a result of her journey through grief, depression, and the near destruction of her marriage, Michelle has had the privilege of holding space for those who are in various trials, leading them into a deep healing and transformation in Christ. As a daughter of the King, wife to her earthly king, professional pastoral counselor, adjunct professor, teacher, speaker, and author, Michelle provides counsel and care through her two greatest passions: helping those who are hurting and teaching others how to help those who are hurting.

Michelle Dickens has been married to her king, Preston Dickens, since 1997! Their three children, Alexis, Joshua, and Bryanna, reside in heaven with Jesus, waiting for the day they can all reunite eternally! Preston retired from the US Air Force after twenty-one years of service and will soon retire from service in the Federal Government. Living out the call on his life, Preston disciples men in one-on-one and small group settings and loves helping out church bands by playing the bass.

"You are the light of the world. A city that is set on a hill cannot be hidden. Neither do men light a candle and put it under a basket, but on a candlestick. And it gives light to all who are in the house. Let your light so shine before men that they may see your good works and glorify your Father who is in heaven."

MATTHEW 5:14–16, (MEV)

Life Under the Microscope: Being a City Set on a Hill

DR. JOSHUA AND RANDEE STEINKE

Testimony Three

Life Under the Microscope: Being a City Set on a Hill

By Dr. Joshua and Randee Steinke

*L*et's be real for a moment—we are a bit wild. We've got a big family, we homeschool, and Wild Willows Homestead is home to approximately 120 animals. I run a busy chiropractic clinic, lead a street ministry (Worship Anyway), write books and songs, and am the lead pastor of our growing church. Oh, and I'm deeply involved with the Christian Chamber of Commerce, promoting kingdom business. Randee, my beautiful bride, codirects a local Christian homeschool group, serves as a 4-H advisor, and coordinates the children's ministry at our church. In many ways, we have chosen to have our life and family on display, and that's not always easy.

In a world filled with distractions and chaos, we have felt a strong call to shine—not just for ourselves but for everyone around us—and let our love, faith, and actions be a light for others, one that can't be hidden, no matter how hard we try. And let's be honest, some days it's hard to remember that. Living under the microscope, with everything feeling exposed and vulnerable, can make you want to pull back and keep your light dimmed. But that's not what Jesus told us to do.

Dr. Joshua's Voice:

The Beginning

We met in college at Ohio Wesleyan University—two small-town track-and-field athletes with big dreams. Randee wanted to work with the Budweiser Clydesdales and travel with their team, while I couldn't decide whether to pursue a medical degree or become a professional choreographer. We both shared a love for animals and community but had no idea where those passions would lead.

After graduation, life took us in different directions. I moved to Marietta, Georgia, to attend chiropractic school, and Randee stayed behind in Ohio to finish her last year of school. But during that year apart, everything began to change. I found a group of friends who had a huge impact on my life. They invited me to Bible studies and worship nights, and over time, God's presence softened my heart. When Randee visited, I started talking more about God than my own plans. During one of those gatherings, in a powerful encounter with the Holy Spirit, both of our hearts were radically transformed. Our passions once focused on worldly goals, suddenly shifted toward Jesus.

> *Our passions once focused on worldly goals, suddenly shifted toward Jesus.*

2 Corinthians 5:17 (MEV) reminds us: *"If any man is in Christ, he is a new creature. Old things have passed away. Look, all things have become new."* We both experienced that firsthand. Our hearts were changed as we encountered the love of God.

A few months later, we knew we had to make a decision. Just one week before our wedding in 2010, we were baptized together in a muddy lake in Georgia, surrounded by those same friends. At that moment, we said "I do" not just to each other but to a new life of transformation, commitment, and service to Jesus. We said "I do" to a calling we couldn't fully see at the time but one that would soon become everything.

> Romans 6:4 (MEV) speaks to the new life we have in Christ, saying, *"Therefore we were buried with Him by baptism into death, that just as Christ was raised up from the dead by the glory of the Father, even so we also should walk in newness of life."*

The Start of a New Journey Together

On the day we said "I do," it felt like it was just us, wrapped up in promises to each other. Hand in hand, we made vows that felt as solid as the ground beneath us. There was something deeper in that moment—a promise not just to each other but to God. We didn't fully understand it then, but we were agreeing to let our love be something bigger, something that would point back to Him.

We were called to be a city set on a hill—to be visible, even when it felt uncomfortable, and to love boldly, even when the world didn't understand. And above all, we were to let our light shine—not for our glory but so others could see the goodness of God through us. It's a journey we're on together, learning as we go and trusting that our light, even when it feels small, makes a difference.

> Ephesians 5:8 (MEV) encourages us, saying, *"For you were formerly darkness, but now you are light in the Lord. Walk as children of light."*

The Early Years

This journey began in the early years of our marriage. We moved back to my hometown to begin building a natural, holistic life together. With very little money and big dreams, we opened our chiropractic practice from scratch. We wanted to create a community that believed in the healing power of God and the natural tools He's given us instead of relying solely on the modern medicine model.

Simple things, like going to the grocery store, became moments when we felt the eyes of others upon us. As a local chiropractor, people would eye our cart and wonder, "Is his wife walking the walk?" It felt like they were waiting for any inconsistency or contradiction between what we said and how we lived. We never expected this kind of scrutiny, but it became part of our reality once we said "I do" to each other and to God's calling on our lives.

> James 1:22 (MEV) tells us to *"Be doers of the word and not hearers only, deceiving yourselves."* Our lives needed to match our faith, even in the small things, like grocery shopping.

The "COVID years" really brought this challenge to a head. We strongly believed our bodies were beautifully made in God's image and that we should steward our health, trusting that we could overcome illness naturally and without fear. We stood firm on that message, even when it didn't align with the public narrative. This put our family and our business under a huge spotlight. We faced threats and messages trying to shame us for being so outwardly bold in our beliefs, and there were times we wondered if we should keep going.

> Romans 8:31 (MEV) reassures us: *"What then shall we say to these things? If God is for us, who can be against us?"* Despite the pushback, we knew we were walking in His will.

Looking back, we can clearly see how God used those struggles to make our light shine brighter. During those difficult years, we saw massive growth in our practice, which necessitated hiring another doctor to share the workload. God opened doors for us to speak about faith and health to people across the country, and my street ministry, Worship Anyway, was solidified during this time. What had been a once- or twice-a-year gathering with a couple hundred people turned into a community-wide movement. The more we stood for our freedom to worship without restriction, the more lives we saw activated to do the same. Unfortunately, this also brought a lot of persecution into our lives. Like many other people who took a stand for freedom during that time, we received many hateful comments and were labeled as "unloving" and "superspreaders." We recall receiving messages before our worship events that accused us of "killing people" because we were drawing large crowds. Some of our friends even sent us messages that questioned our actions and intentions. The story from Acts 16, where Paul and Silas sang while locked in a dungeon, continued to be our encouragement. We felt strongly that we were called to live out the message "No matter what life brings, worship anyway!" That message has carried us through and continues to be our heartfelt message today. We have witnessed so many people encouraged by that message locally, statewide, nationally, and even internationally, making it clear the Lord knew what He was doing through it all.

2 Corinthians 4:8–9 (MEV) speaks to how we can shine despite hardship, saying, *"We are troubled on every side, yet not distressed; we are perplexed, but not in despair; persecuted, but not forsaken; cast down, but not destroyed."*

Randee's Voice:

Growing Our Family

Joshua and I made the decision to have all our babies at home. It was a different path that the people around us didn't always understand. Especially with our first couple of births, people questioned why we didn't follow the "traditional" route and scrutinized every choice we made. We chose to question everything that seemed "status quo" for birth, and that didn't sit well with many.

During our second birth, I hemorrhaged severely after delivery. While the baby was perfectly fine, our midwife decided we needed to go to the hospital due to my blood loss. After a tense visit, which almost led to Joshua being arrested, we made it home with minimal intervention. This situation opened the door for even more questions, but it also became an opportunity for us to show God's goodness once again. We've used that story to encourage others when things didn't go exactly as planned, reminding them that God still works it out when we trust Him. I have had so many opportunities to counsel other expectant moms who needed empowerment to make the decisions they really desired.

> Romans 8:28 (MEV) assures us that *"All things work together for good to those who love God, to those who are called according to His purpose."* Even in the midst of trials, we see how God worked it out.

Giving birth wasn't the only area where we've gone against the grain. From the moment our children entered the world, we made choices based on what felt right for our family, not popular opinion. We chose not to have ultrasounds—not because we thought they couldn't be helpful but because we never felt the need for them. Likewise, we opted out of newborn screenings and vaccinations. We've always trusted holistic approaches to health, treating our kids with chiropractic care, supplements, herbs, essential oils, and lots of good food and rest. We have continued to preach that the body really is beautifully and wonderfully created in the image of

God and that God doesn't create junk! Because of how we've lived and the fruit of our family members' lives, we've had the privilege of helping many families seeking answers for their own health journeys.

> Proverbs 3:5–6 (MEV) reminds us to *"Trust in the Lord with all your heart, and lean not on your own understanding; in all your ways acknowledge Him, and He will direct your paths."* Trusting God's way, even when it's unconventional, has been key.

As our kids grew, we faced another decision: schooling. We sent our oldest to public kindergarten, like most parents do. But after that first year, I felt strongly that God was calling me to homeschool. It wasn't an easy decision, especially since Joshua's family has deep roots in public education. We didn't have anything against public school; we just knew God was leading us to teach our kids at home, and we wanted to follow that call. Homeschooling has been one of the greatest challenges and one of the greatest blessings of our lives. Sometimes, it feels like it would be less frustrating for me just to send the kids to public school. But every time we've questioned the decision, God has reaffirmed it. I've been able to use both the highs and lows of homeschooling to minister to other moms, encouraging them to stick with it through the challenges.

> Deuteronomy 6:6–7 (MEV) speaks to our role as parents in teaching our children, saying, *"These words, which I am commanding you today, shall be in your heart. You shall teach them diligently to your children and shall talk of them when you sit in your house, and when you walk by the way, and when you lie down, and when you rise up."*

Living Our Faith Loud

Since that powerful encounter with Jesus during chiropractic school, we've felt a strong calling to boldly share the message of Jesus everywhere we go. We've always viewed our chiropractic office more as a ministry than a business. For years, I served as office manager, sharing the love of Jesus with everyone who walked in while Joshua prayed for the sick and watched them recover. Our office culture has always been one of worship and joy, creating a place of refuge for those who need it. Along the way, we've also worked hard to debunk the idea that a husband and wife can't thrive while working together!

Being loud about Jesus can be scary when you own a small business. We've lost patients and friends and faced much criticism over the years. We've been uninvited from places and asked to quiet down. We've even lost money. But despite all of that, we've seen thousands of lives changed because of it. In recent years, we began to rally and encourage other people and Jesus-loving business owners to be loud about their faith in the business sector. This has created an opportunity for kingdom collaboration in business and ministry as well as friendships all over the country! If you had asked us in college if we'd ever be evangelists in the marketplace, we would have thought you were crazy!

> Romans 1:16 (MEV) says, *"For I am not ashamed of the gospel of Christ. For it is the power of God for salvation to everyone who believes, to the Jew first, and also to the Greek."*

Answering the Call

The scrutiny increased significantly when Joshua became the lead pastor of our church. Suddenly, it wasn't just our family under the microscope—it was everything we did. I was hesitant at first. I didn't feel like I fit the mold of a "pastor's wife." In fact, I had even been told I wouldn't be a good "pastor's wife." The pressure was immense for me and for our kids as well.

Pastors' kids often face a higher standard when perfection is expected, and there's little room for mistakes. Joshua and I didn't want that extra pressure on our kids, especially after all the challenges we'd already faced. The thought of living under even more scrutiny felt overwhelming. But the more we embraced the calling, the more we realized the importance of living out our faith authentically—not for the approval of others but to honor the One who called us.

> *But the more we embraced the calling, the more we realized the importance of living out our faith authentically— not for the approval of others but to honor the One who called us.*

> Galatians 1:10 (MEV) reminds us: *"For am I now seeking the approval of men or of God? Or am I trying to please men? For if I were still trying to please men, I would not be the servant of Christ."*

Worth It All

One last encouraging story to bring this all full circle. In the last few years, Joshua and I have felt we should bring all aspects of being "salt and light to the earth" together under one roof. As we were praying through what that might look like, we were quickly given this vision of "Organic Momma," which became a gathering we hosted for several hundred women (and men) who desired to live life in ways similar to ours. We were able to bring natural health, parenting, home birth, worship, ministry, fellowship, wise counsel, and Jesus under one roof to encourage and equip families and marriages. We were able to see a like-minded and on-fire community of families come together and be ignited to do the same thing we had been doing. Thank you, Jesus!

So, [Dr. Joshua here] why do we choose to live this way? After all, when we married in 2010, we had no idea what saying "I do" would mean for our marriage in all of these various aspects. Is it worth it? Absolutely. There have been times when Randee has wondered, "Can't we just fly under the radar?" or "When do we get to show up late and sit in the back?" Maybe one day we will. But most likely, that day will come when we enter heaven and hear the words "Well done, good and faithful servant." Until then, we count it an honor to be a light in the darkness. The lives changed, the people coming to know Jesus, the families being healed, and the believers being activated to live a life on fire for the Lord—those are the rewards. As the apostle Paul said, "For me to live is Christ, and to die is gain" (Philippians 1:21, ESV). Every part of our lives is laid down, even if we didn't realize we were saying "I do" to it, because Jesus is worthy of it all!

> Matthew 25:23 (MEV) says, *"His master said to him, 'Well done, you good and faithful servant. You have been faithful over a few things. I will make you ruler over many things. Enter the joy of your master.'"*

Life Under the Microscope: Being a City Set on a Hill

DR. JOSHUA AND RANDEE STEINKE

For Her: When you said "I do" and committed to sharing life with your spouse, what aspects of your life became unexpectedly exposed? How could you leverage this to bring your marriage together?

For Him: At times, you may be called to take on something in life that your wife isn't personally called to. How can you encourage her to join you in that journey, and what steps can you take to shield her if she feels uncomfortable or overwhelmed by the exposure that comes with it?

For Yourself: How can your marriage reflect the idea of a "city on a hill?" What impact could that have on the people around you, both positive and negative?

Ask One Another

Take time to prayerfully ask one another these questions, seeking God's guidance to grow together.

Dr. Joshua Steinke is a devoted father of eight and the loving husband of Mrs. Randee Steinke. As a chiropractor, he is deeply committed to healing the body and the spirit. Dr. Joshua is the director of Worship Anyway, a street outreach ministry focused on spreading the message of Jesus in the community. In addition, he serves as the lead pastor at Living Hope Worship Center in St. Mary's, Ohio. He is also an author and a songwriter, using his gifts to encourage others in their walk of faith.

Randee Steinke, a mother of eight and wife to Dr. Joshua, is dedicated to nurturing her family and empowering others. She directs Wild Willows Homestead, where she teaches her children and other families how to live in harmony with God's design. Passionate about homeschooling, Randee also codirects a local Christian homeschool group, helping families grow in faith and knowledge through Christ-centered education.

Together, Dr. Joshua and Randee are united in their mission to lay hands on the sick and watch them recover, worship God in every season, and restore hope to their communities through the transformative power of Jesus Christ.

"In the same way, you wives, be submissive to your own husbands [subordinate, not as inferior, but out of respect for the responsibilities entrusted to husbands and their accountability to God, and so partnering with them] so that even if some do not obey the word [of God], they may be won over [to Christ] without discussion by the godly lives of their wives, when they see your modest and respectful behavior [together with your devotion and appreciation—love your husband, encourage him, and enjoy him as a blessing from God]."

1 PETER 3:1–2, AMP

Unequally Yoked: Breaking Idols and Buiding Husbands

JENNIFER BEEMAN

Testimony Four

Unequally Yoked:
Breaking Idols and Building Husbands

By Jennifer Beeman

Building Idols

We had shared more than ten years of friendship and just over one year of marriage. We were accustomed to dealing with one another in difficult situations: I stressed him until he gave up and remained noncombative . . . then I got my way. It was how we rolled, until now, that is. Once again, we were battling another set of landlords. We had lived in this house for about a month and a half, and a series of minor issues had accumulated into a massive problem. The landlords neglected their end of the agreement, and we neglected ours. No one was right, but my hubby was ready to take vengeance against what he perceived as a personal insult to our character. At this point in our relationship, we had no concept of biblical leadership or how a relationship should function. We were both from broken homes and thought that making it this far was a big deal. I allowed him to make decisions and guide our family, but only as long as all my criteria were met. I thrived on the illusion of control.

So, even though we agreed this living situation was not a good match, I viewed our circumstances with different eyes. In my alone time with God, I was learning the importance of treating those who mistreat you as though they were appointed to you by God. They were to be treated with care and consideration. After all, how would they recognize grace if they didn't have the chance to receive it? When we initially arrived at this place, it was dirty and overrun by spiders. We had two toddlers who were into everything, and having no other choice at the time, I leaned into the work. Tensions increased further when we were informed the position my hubby was promised was no longer available. He would now have to travel five days a week and be three hours away from us with our only vehicle.

The strain on our time, patience, finances, and parenting was intense. So when it all caved in, we were already exhausted. Looking back now, we see that nothing was wasted. It was during episodes of *Curious George* and toddler naps that I was able to dive into God's Word. Jesus was continuing the sanctification work He had begun the year prior. As I shared in the book *Before She Knew Jesus*, God had started me on this journey with a lesson in forgiveness, and now He was about to reveal how to identify idols, what to do about them, and just how much He loves it when we trust Him.

During this time, it was revealed to me that I was holding my husband hostage to my unchecked needs, needs he was not meant to meet outside of healing and the sanctification process with Jesus. The beautiful truth about this process is that Jesus does not hide His expectations of how we should live. He provides full disclosure. He prompts and guides us toward creating a tender heart within us that sees people, not just their actions.

Although we had come to a mutual agreement to move out of the house, there was a moment of heated discussion about the way we should handle the situation. While I firmly believed that both parties were wrong and we needed to handle this with respect, my hubby was not in agreement. He had been wronged and believed that it no longer mattered what we had done, only that they got what they deserved. I was usually in agreement, uniting with him in the offense and minimizing our responsibility in any given situation. We often held the belief that we were perpetual victims. This was a pivotal moment, however, one where we were not pulling the yoke of our marriage in the same direction. Although we had grown up knowing about the truth of Jesus, neither one of us truly *loved* the truth of Jesus. But now that my heart was softening, it changed how I responded to life. I didn't fully understand all the concepts or accept all the ways God loved me. The truth was that I often questioned my worthiness to accept His love, but Jesus continued to gently reassure me of my true and ultimate identity as a child of God.

We had barely finished packing the last of the house into the pull trailer when the argument began. I expressed my plan to give the place a deep cleaning and repair everything I could find. This meant my hubby would need to care for the kids and let me clean. He expressed his frustration and feelings about my plans, and I took his words and used them to build a garden of resentment. I replayed in my mind all the things he did that irritated me. Each seed was tended with care and effort to ensure it was nursed and validated. And as they germinated, they began to wrap their roots of bitterness around my heart.

He hung around inside the house as I began to clean, his mere presence meant to push me along to finish the task faster. As an additional assault on my dedication to the task, he began making side comments, such as "Mommy is wasting her time" and "They didn't care; why should we?" The momma bear in me was roused at the thought that he would place my choice to honor others as a negative in the minds of my children. I quietly resolved to continue cleaning through the comments. God had told me to clean, so that's what I did. God did not tell me to tend the garden of resentments; I did that all on my own. In a rare moment of gumption, I stood up from the dirt-covered floor (body shaking and voice cracking) to say, "My goal is to be as blameless as possible. I'm tired of being the guilty one. I will do what God asked, regardless of what you think. I can get this done quicker if you would just leave me alone." An exchange of words like that was rare between us, and his response was to gather the kids and wait in the truck.

In my feelings, I cried out with silent prayers: "Why won't he just do what he sees is the right thing to do?" What I know now but did not understand then was that he *couldn't* see the right thing to do. That was the point; he needed to love Jesus too. The dynamics of our relationship leaned heavily on my leadership. I was the one who focused more on the results at the end of a situation than on my feelings in the middle of it. When Jesus changed the narrative in my heart, it shifted my allegiance to Him and away from destructive thinking.

> *That was the point; he needed to love Jesus too.*

Unequally Yoked

If you are around Christian circles long enough, you will eventually hear the term "unequally yoked." Second Corinthians 6:14–15 (NIV) says, "Do not be yoked together with unbelievers. For what do righteousness and wickedness have in common? Or what fellowship can light have with darkness? . . . Or what does a believer have in common with an unbeliever?" But what if you're *already* married? The Bible warns us against being unequally yoked with an unbeliever in marriage, and technically, we hadn't done so. We had checked the boxes of *our* religion. We believed in the story of Jesus, accepted His forgiveness, and were baptized. We were playing married before we were married. Our wedding date and the ages of our kids didn't equate to purity before marriage. The difference now was that I understood what a relationship with Jesus meant. I was experiencing His redeeming grace and endless mercy. I wanted that truth for my hubby as well.

The phrase "unequally yoked" indicates those in partnership have different values or goals. This will eventually lead to conflict, with one or both partners making an unhealthy compromise. A healthy compromise is one in which both partners give a little and arrive at a solution that is mutually agreed upon or beneficial. An unhealthy compromise occurs when one person sacrifices their values to please the other. We truly believed that getting married would undo the years we willingly lived in sin, but we were both continuing to make unhealthy compromises. This led us to knowingly neglect placing our relationship with Jesus before our relationship with each other.

> *A healthy compromise is one in which both partners give a little and arrive at a solution that is mutually agreed upon or beneficial.*

Why Does It Matter?

What is the harm in being bound to another in the "yoke" of an unequal relationship? It all comes down to purpose. The purpose of a yoke is to disperse the weight of the workload. Spreading the weight across the shoulders makes reaching the goal more attainable, but this is only possible if both are equally matched and leaning into the same goal. The yoke also represents the concept of submission. To keep moving forward, the ox must occasionally lean into the yoke, spurring its partner to advance as well. These seemingly small acts of submission improve the quality of the experience for all involved. In our relationship with God, it means setting aside our will for God's will.

In the most common interpretation of the yoke analogy, we are told to use a team of oxen that are similar in size. If a farmer chooses animals of different sizes, the load they bear will be uneven, causing the yoke to rub against their skin. The constant rubbing can cause pain and raw sores to develop, and the animals will begin to compromise their stance and adjust to avoid discomfort. This change in stance will put the animals at risk of causing serious injury to one another. Even if no physical damage is observed, the ability to move forward in a straight line will be impacted. The team will end up walking in circles, thus avoiding the goal altogether. We do this in our relationships as well. We often compromise in unhealthy ways to avoid the pain of rejection or conflict. Our goal should be to know God intimately and learn how to love others, but by compromising our values, we create confusion and discord among those looking to us for an example of Jesus.

Breaking Idols

The landlords were so impressed with the cleaning that they returned half of our deposit (which we didn't deserve). I spent the months afterward sharing with my hubby all the ways we had gone wrong. I figured the outcome would spur him on to greater works! I was wrong. With my strength and brilliant planning, I envisioned how we would work together to have the biblical marriage needed for our children. Instead, I ended up mentally and emotionally exhausted as I poured out everything I was taking in. To his credit, he never stopped me when I told him all I was learning. But I wondered why he couldn't understand the wisdom I was sharing. After months of talking until I was out of breath, it became clear that no amount of talking was making a difference—the same broken thought processes were in play, with little change. What could I do to get him to realize what I already knew? I knew it was important for us to align our relationship with the Word of God, but how could we make that happen? It was then that God revealed I had made my husband and idol. Rustin Rossello says that if you have the thought, "I can't unless they . . ." then you have made them an idol. During those early years, I had told myself, "I can't make that choice unless he . . ." But now that I had identified the problem, where did I go from here?

The Lord heard my plea, and as if on cue, I found myself listening to a radio program by Chuck Swindoll called *Insight For Living*. I remember hearing him say, "At very unique junctures of our lives, God says to us, 'Now, My child, I have this in mind for you. I know that you have knotted things up in the past. And I know that you may knot things up in the future. But as far as today, right now, this is My plan for you. Now go. I'm sending you, and I will be with you.'"

That was all I needed to continue this journey. God was so incredibly sweet to lead me in loosening my grip. He spoke with me through His Word in verses such as Matthew 11:28–30 (NIV): "Come to me, all you who are weary and burdened, and I will give you rest. Take my yoke upon you and learn from me, for I am gentle and humble in heart, and you will find rest for your souls. For my yoke is easy and my burden is light" and Habakkuk 1:5 (NIV): "Look at the nations and watch—and be utterly amazed. For I am going to do something in your days that you would not believe, even if you were told." God wanted me to loosen the grip on my husband, and He lifted one stubborn finger at a time until my will for my husband was left sitting exposed and powerless in the palm of my hand. It was then that I conceded, "Lord, I can't fix him. Only you can do that. Show me how."

Quit Talking and Keep Doing

I knew my source for moving forward needed to come from Scripture. It was the only sure thing I could trust in a season when everything was changing. The verse I clung to the most provides guidance in situations like mine.

> "In the same way, you wives, be submissive to your own husbands [subordinate, not as inferior, but out of respect for the responsibilities entrusted to husbands and their accountability to God, and so partnering with them] so that even if some do not obey the word [of God], they may be won over [to Christ] without discussion by the godly lives of their wives, when they see your modest and respectful behavior [together with your devotion and appreciation—love your husband, encourage him, and enjoy him as a blessing from God]" (1 Peter 3:1–2, AMP).

I hear you loud and clear, Lord! I was to *show* him through example. I often looked for moments to include him in a godly example. One such time involved some difficult choices we faced concerning what groceries we could afford. We had placed many non-essentials in our cart and needed to put some back. Instead of allowing the items to be unloaded on the closest shelf, I walked us back to where we had initially picked up each item. His response was not positive, but I smiled and emphasized it was the respectful thing to do. Afterward, I was equipped with the Word formed into prayers.

Here are my personal favorites:

1. Father, give my husband the mind of Christ; saturate it with godly wisdom. Help him to take every thought captive that is not in obedience to Your Word, and in so doing, protect him from pride and temptation (1 Corinthians 2:16, 2 Corinthians 10:5).
2. Father, open the eyes of my husband's heart to understand your Word so that he won't be conformed to this world but will be transformed by the renewing of his mind. I ask that he may know your good, acceptable, and perfect will for his life and our marriage (Romans 12:2).

It took about three months of dedication to prayer and surrender before I started to see a change in his actions and words. In addition to the prayers and Scripture, I was learning to bring my specific requests to God for safekeeping. This practice gave space for the Lord to work while I waited. I was astonished one day when I asked Jesus to hold me. I knew I was going to need holy restraint if I was to lovingly remind the hubby that the girls did not *need* new toys and that he simply *wanted* them to have new toys. I was stressed about finances and was still learning how to compromise in a healthy way when it came to money. The shocking moment occurred when he arrived home and said, "The girls do have too many toys, and we can't even keep things cleaned up as they are." *Uh, what was that you said?* He repeated himself, and I giggled at this undeniable proof that God was on the move! He looked at me like I had lost my mind, not knowing if he should be happy or worried. I repeated this practice countless times. It didn't take long before he caught on that something was different. He asked why I kept laughing at him, as it made him feel uncomfortable. I explained that I got tired of telling him what I wanted and decided to give it to a man who would listen! Shortly thereafter, he began to put the cart back in the cart rack with no reminder! He was talking about the church service, even after we left. He was asking me questions and truly wanted answers. This was all so strange, new, and exciting. Thank you, Jesus!

We Toil Together (Our "I Do" Now)

Our first few years of "I do" were characterized by power struggles, questions, and forgiveness. We have been married for eleven years now, and God has grown us both in the areas of grace, forgiveness, and relational wisdom. We are still practicing biblical leadership within the family unit and have taken ownership of our relationships with God, meeting with Jesus daily. We have become accustomed to holding our lives before the Lord with an open hand and working together, spurring each other on to growth and intimacy in Christ. When we were going through our toughest struggles, we lacked community, especially an active community of believers. Getting plugged into a local church was the key to success. We learned that having a community of individuals willing to engage in difficult conversations and call out the truth is a precious gift from the Lord.

> *We have become accustomed to holding our lives before the Lord with an open hand and working together, spurring each other on to growth and intimacy in Christ.*

In an interview with my husband, he reflected on our journey from his point of view. Here are some points he wanted to share:

1. Take a deep breath. God is most likely trying to help *you* through *her*. Listen closely to what she is saying and observe what she is doing. The differences are where the growth will be. God is dedicated to reaching you.
2. When asked what the most impactful moment was during this time in our relationship, he shared, "The moment that caught my attention was when she told me she was done sharing what she was learning. She told me I was not listening and God needed her to step back from this part of our relationship. She continued to display the behavior God asked her to exhibit, but she was not bringing up the subject of God with me. That was the moment I knew God was real and active. He was not the God of my childhood."
3. Take a moment to get quiet and ask what is hindering you from connecting with God.

Unequally Yoked: Breaking Idols and Building Husbands

JENNIFER BEEMAN

Ask Her: Is there any place in our relationship where you feel my actions or words make you feel underappreciated?

Ask Him: What are some behaviors or choices I make that result in you feeling disrespected?

Ask Yourself: Where am I struggling to surrender to God?

Ask One Another

Take time to prayerfully ask one another these questions, seeking God's guidance to grow together.

Jennifer is a passionate author, speaker, and storyteller who is dedicated to strengthening marriages and inspiring faith. A proud wife to her husband, Andrew, Jennifer draws from her own experiences and spiritual journey to encourage others in their relationships and walk with Christ.

She is a best-selling author in Before She Knew Jesus, a transformative book that has touched countless lives with its message of redemption and grace. When she's not writing, Jennifer serves as a barista at her church café, where she loves connecting with the community over a cup of coffee.

Jennifer also hosts the popular podcast Stories of a Faith Builder, where she shares heartfelt conversations and uplifting testimonies that inspire listeners to deepen their faith and trust in God.

Whether through her writing, podcasting, or personal interactions, Jennifer's mission is to build stronger marriages and help others grow closer to Christ.

"Therefore what God has joined together, let no one separate."

MARK 10:9, NIV

Wounded, Weary, and Worth Fighting For: A Marriage Redemption Story

STEVE AND KESS SCHARFF

Testimony Five

Wounded, Weary, and Worth Fighting For: A Marriage Redemption Story

By Steve and Kess Scharff

Introduction: The Battle for Marriage

When we revisit the story of Eve in the garden of Eden, it's easy to oversimplify what happened. Many of us may read Genesis and flippantly think, "Well, Eve trusted Satan, and Adam just went along with it." But let's pause and really break this down. How would Satan, a fallen angel, even be allowed into the garden—a place designed to be perfect and sinless? And why would Eve, living in paradise, obey him?

This ancient story mirrors much of what we face in marriage today. Straying from commitment, whether through infidelity, addiction, or neglect, is rarely an abrupt decision. Instead, it's the gradual buying into lies—lies that tell us happiness is the ultimate goal, that our spouse should change to meet our needs, or that love is purely transactional.

Marriage was designed to reflect God's covenant love. It's about becoming one flesh, working as a team with shared goals, and living in a way that reflects Jesus to the world. It's not easy; it's the hardest and most rewarding work you'll ever do. The beauty of marriage lies in surrender: surrendering our pride, our need to control, and our brokenness to God while trusting Him to shape us into the people He designed us to be. In *Love and War,* John Eldredge invites us to consider a powerful truth: What if God designed marriage not just for companionship but for transformation? What if marriage, like the garden of Eden, is intended to refine us, shaping us into the people He created us to be? Eldredge suggests we are drawn together by divine intention—as helpmates—not just to support each other but to grow together in love, grace, and faith. Could the very challenges we face in marriage be part of God's greater plan to make us more like Christ?

When Love Became Action: His Story

Two days after arriving at college, an angel appeared to me.

She was five feet one inch tall with brown hair. Her skin was tanned from the summer sun, and she looked amazing in her white cutoff jean shorts and purple tank top. I immediately knew I needed to know her.

The more I got to know her, the more I wanted to be with her. I was in love!

We began spending more time together and eventually decided to start dating. It was then that I learned about the horrible experiences from her past and how she had been sexually abused for most of her eighteen years. I felt so badly for her and what she had gone through. I was angry and confused, and I wasn't sure what I was supposed to do. I knew I wanted to confront those who hurt her, but she told me she wanted it to remain a secret. This was a crossroads. I wanted to be the knight in shining armor and protect her like a man was "supposed" to do, but I also wanted to show her I was trustworthy. I didn't want to lose her, so I swallowed my pride and kept her secret.

Over time, issues began to pop up that stemmed from her trauma. I decided I would learn as much as possible about the impacts of sexual abuse by reading every book I could find. I had come to the conclusion that she was "broken," and I was going to fix her.

We had amazing times and horrible times. I didn't understand what I was doing wrong. I was putting all my efforts into making Kess feel loved and happy, but nothing stuck. The harder I tried, the more difficult it became. This cycle continued through our engagement and into our marriage.

We graduated from college, landed good jobs, and had a beautiful wedding. We had made it. Life was going to be incredible now. And, honestly, it was . . . for a little while. As life progressed, however, more and more of Kess's past traumas came pouring out, and the more that poured out, the more I tried to fix her.

The first time she mentioned divorce was when we disagreed on the number of children we wanted. She told me if I wasn't going to give her what she wanted, she would leave me and find another man who would. *What did she just say to me?* I heard that I was worthless to her unless I gave her what she wanted. This rocked me to my core because it echoed the message I was told growing up.

Years of manipulation started. She would twist my words to make them sound the way she wanted them to sound. Whenever she wanted something different from what I wanted, she would withhold things or make threats until she got her way. I was in a bad place. I became angry, withdrew emotionally from our marriage, and started to focus more on my career, where I had accomplishments and was appreciated. The problem was that I had to go home every night, and I didn't like being at home. I would pull up to our house and have panic attacks in my car before going in. My heart would start racing, and I would break out in cold sweats. This went on for years.

During this time, I became very resentful and angry, but I found that hanging out with friends and drinking helped distract me from my problems . . . at least the problem of having to go home each night. When I was home, I wanted to be left alone. I would lash out and become easily angered when confronted. I didn't feel like anything was my fault, and I was tired of taking the blame.

Success continued at work, bringing on a number of new opportunities that moved us around the country. These moves became distractions that would start off nicely but eventually cycle back to misery. I was looking for ways to escape my pain, so I continued to work more, hang out with friends more, and drink more. I became more and more angry and resentful. I couldn't believe I was doing so much good while she was screwing everything up. What happened to that angel I met in college?

Divorce threats continued to be thrown around. We started living in separate bedrooms but hid this from our girls. I was in so much pain! I remember spending one Saturday looking at townhomes, and I broke down in tears while talking to the real estate agent. I don't cry! Men aren't supposed to show weakness, and crying is weakness. What in the world was wrong with me?

We had started attending churches a few years before, but nothing was really clicking for me. I had grown up with religion but not faith. I didn't understand there was supposed to be a relationship with God. The Bible was a holy object we weren't supposed to touch, and church was a place we went to on Christmas and Easter. I thought "church people" were weird.

One Sunday at church, after my breakdown with the real estate agent, I saw an advertisement for a Christian marriage conference. I decided Kess and I needed to go. I thought for sure she would jump at this opportunity, but I was wrong again. She didn't want to go and felt I was trying to manipulate her to change her mind about divorce. But for some reason, I knew I needed to attend that conference with or without her.

Thankfully, Kess ended up going with me. During the conference, we were split into separate training sessions. In the session for husbands, the speaker was a redheaded pastor from Alaska. I don't remember much of his teaching, but at one point, he looked out into the audience of 300 men and asked if anyone felt lost and didn't know what to do. He asked if we had been trying to fill the emptiness in our hearts with things like alcohol, porn, partying, etc. He then said these words: "Try plugging the love of Jesus Christ into that empty place in your heart and see how that fits." I didn't even know what that meant, but it felt as though my heart exploded. My body went numb and tingled all over. I felt a peace I had never felt before. I couldn't wait to share this strange experience with Kess, but when I did during the next break, she wasn't as excited about it as I was. She had checked out and was done with me.

During the next session, that same pastor challenged us to go home that night and pray with our wives. This was as foreign to me as being told to go home and speak Greek to my wife. That night, however, I took him up on his challenge. I prayed for us. I prayed for our marriage. I prayed for our family. I prayed with my wife—out loud!

We went back for day two, and I was now all in. I went right up to the front row and found a seat. Sure enough, the Alaskan ginger was on stage again. He asked if any of us had taken his challenge. I had, so I raised my hand. He looked down at me and asked if I really did. I looked around and realized that of the 300 men in the room, I was the only one with my hand raised. He called me up on stage, and he and the other men prayed over my marriage. What in the world was going on? My head was spinning, but I felt some clarity for the first time in a long time.

I would love to say everything miraculously changed and that we lived happily ever after. But that would be a lie. Miracles did happen, though. I started a relationship with Jesus and began to learn what it meant to be a Christian man and husband. I realized I was trying to control things and fix them on my own. Kess had experienced horrible trauma in her life, and she brought significant baggage into our relationship. However, I had baggage of my own and realized I needed to work on myself instead of trying to fix Kess. I began joining Bible studies and seeking counseling. Everything was going pretty well for years until, suddenly, it wasn't.

> *I started a relationship with Jesus and began to learn what it meant to be a Christian man and husband.*

Kess began treatment at an outpatient program for behavioral health, and everything seemed out of control again. Our conversations became very irrational, and I didn't know what was going on. It started to feel like we were reliving the past. I fell back into my protection modes from earlier in our marriage, and instead of turning to Jesus, I turned to work, friends, and drinking once again. Rather than dealing with what was happening, I avoided it, and I felt like a failure.

At this point, my counselor suggested that I was showing traits of codependence, and this could add to the hardships we were both facing in our marriage. I found a Christian support group, which helped me to see weakness and failure differently. Weakness is being too proud to accept your issues and realize you need help. Failure is not getting that help.

I started to study the Bible more and gained a better understanding of God's love. This helped me through tremendous trials in my life and our marriage. I began to understand why Jesus had to die for my sins and how, through His sacrifice, my past mistakes and sins were forgiven by God. I became more comfortable with this idea but realized I was not forgiving myself. I was basically telling God it was okay for Him to forgive me, but it wasn't okay for me to forgive myself.

I battled with this for a while before a recruiter contacted me and offered me a high-level executive position with a company. It was an amazing opportunity and proof that others saw value in me. To make it even better, the company claimed to be faith-based and would only offer the job to someone they felt was living an honorable Christian life. Not only was I being told I was good at my job, but I was being told I was good at being a Christian man. I accepted this job, and we moved again.

Not long after moving, Kess tried to take her life. She was admitted to a mental health hospital, and we weren't sure if she would ever fully recover. I was angry, sad, and confused. I felt lost, and I felt betrayed by Kess . . . but also by God. Hadn't we been through enough? Hadn't I proven I was a good Christian man?

I had three daughters to care for and a company to run, so I didn't have time to focus on myself. I kept up the façade for a couple of weeks, but then I broke down. The amazing thing was, when I broke, I went running to God. It is only through Him that I was able to make it through that tragic time. I felt loved in a way I had never felt before. Although I was angry with Kess, I began to feel a deeper love for her. It wasn't that I loved her more; it was that I loved her differently.

We walk through this world with the idea that love is an emotion. We flippantly say we love things like pizza. We fall in love with people, but when things get tough, we quit. That isn't God's definition of love. God's definition of love is a verb. It is an action. It isn't a feeling.

Many have heard 1 Corinthians 13:4–7 (NIV), but have they really paid attention to how God defines love in this verse?

> "Love is patient, love is kind. It does not envy, it does not boast, it is not proud. It does not dishonor others, it is not self-seeking, it is not easily angered, it keeps no record of wrongs. Love does not delight in evil but rejoices with the truth. It always protects, always trusts, always hopes, always perseveres."

This is what I meant by loving her "differently." Despite the struggles in our marriage, the baggage we carried, the attempts to fix each other, and the desire to run away from it all, God had a bigger plan for us. He said it would be more than the attraction I felt when I first saw her. He was with us through everything, even though I didn't realize it. We needed to learn to be patient and kind to ourselves and each other. He wanted us to learn how to honor each other and stop being selfish. It's not about winning the argument; it's about seeing the truth and forgiving each other. With God's definition of love, there can always be protection, trust, and hope. Most importantly, God's definition of love says that it will never give up, no matter how difficult it gets, and it will fight until it overcomes.

Our marriage isn't perfect, but I can say there is more love today than ever before. All of the tough times have led us to where we are today. If I had not put my faith in Jesus years ago, our marriage would have ended in divorce—like the world said it should. Romans 12:2 (NIV) tells us, "Do not conform to the pattern of this world, but be transformed by the renewing of your mind. Then you will be able to test and approve what God's will is—his good, pleasing and perfect will."

Happily Ever After: Her Story

When Steve proposed, it felt like all my dreams were coming true. From the time I was a little girl, I had longed for a fairy-tale life: a perfect wedding, a beautiful marriage, and the promise of happily ever after. I dreamed of a home with a white picket fence, children laughing as they chased our dog, and a love that would finally make me whole. I anchored my happiness to this dream, clinging to the hope his words carried.

I was so desperate for "I do" to be the answer to my longing, the key to unlocking the fairy tale I had always imagined. What I didn't realize about fairy tales, however, was that before the finale of love, there is always a battle—a war fought for the happy ending. I had skipped over that part of the story. I liked the idea of him being my hero, of being rescued, of skipping straight to the part where love triumphed, and of everything being as it should be.

I thought I was ready for my fairy tale. I couldn't have been more wrong.

The Baggage of My Past

Many people enter marriage carrying a suitcase full of emotional baggage, but I brought an entire moving van. It backed up to the altar with its slow, deliberate *beep, beep, beep*, loaded with boxes of unresolved pain, shame, fear, and scars I didn't yet understand.

From the time I was three years old, my world was marked by chaos. I wasn't just a child; I was a survivor before I even knew what survival meant. There were drug runs, motorcycle rides, and homes that changed as quickly as my mother could afford them. Where I lived and who I lived with were ever-changing. Schools changed depending on who could care for me that season. Protection and safety were foreign concepts. Instead, I witnessed violence: doors knocked down and nights spent hiding for our lives. And yet, the same grandmother who was my safe place would send me back to a man whose life revolved around drugs, alcohol, and every form of abuse imaginable.

Peace and protection were concepts I never knew. Love felt dangerous. My very sense of self was shaped by lies I didn't have the words to confront. Sexual abuse doesn't just wound the body; it reaches into the soul, distorting what God created to be good and pure. It replaces innocence with shame, whispering that you are unworthy, broken, and unlovable. And when the abuse comes from the very people meant to protect you, the scars feel impossible to heal.

As I grew older, I learned how to cope—I detached from my body. It was no longer something sacred but something to use, adorn, or manipulate to keep trouble at bay. I didn't realize I was still carrying the cycle of objectification and shame that had started in childhood.

By the time I stood at the altar with Steve, I had convinced myself his love would rescue me. I believed that this marriage, this fairy tale I had constructed in my mind, would somehow fix what was broken inside me.

But no human being could carry the weight of what I had placed on him.

A Marriage Suffocated by Pain

The emotional baggage I brought into our marriage didn't just clutter our lives; it suffocated us! Every box of unresolved trauma and every unspoken fear spilled into the space Steve and I were trying to build together. Our home became so crowded with emotional junk that there was no room to breathe, no space for peace, and no desire for closeness. For Steve, life with me must have felt like navigating a maze of hidden triggers and unmet expectations. Like land mines buried beneath the clutter, he couldn't see them until they exploded.

Steve became the target of my frustration and the face of my pain. I blamed him for not being able to fix what I was too afraid to confront within myself. We both carried our own wounds, but my pain dominated every corner of our lives. I didn't see Steve's efforts to love me. I only saw what I felt was missing. His attempts to reach out felt inadequate against the backdrop of my unresolved struggles, making our relationship feel like a constant battle rather than a partnership.

In trying to survive together, we lost sight of any intimacy or understanding. Simple moments turned into conflicts: "I'm not giving you a hug; you're mean," or "I'm not fully listening; you're nagging." It felt like a constant tit for tat, where neither of us wanted to give unless the other had first filled our emotional cups. But the person who was supposed to nourish me couldn't fill my cup despite their efforts—something that, ironically, had brought us together in the beginning.

The emotional clutter we couldn't clear created walls between us, turning our home into a battleground where love struggled to find its place. Reflecting on our journey, I now realize how deeply my past affected our present and how essential it is to address the baggage we carry if we wish to truly build a life together. I learned I needed to own my responsibility first.

If you've ever felt like you couldn't give your all because your cup was never full, you're not alone. Our story is a reminder that healing ourselves is crucial if we are to nurture the relationships we hold dear.

> "See to it that no one falls short of the grace of God and that no bitter root grows up to cause trouble and defile many" (Hebrews 12:15, NIV).

The Weight of Fear and Shame

The lies I believed fed a relentless fear that I was unlovable and destined to fail. That fear became the foundation of towering walls I built around my heart, walls I thought would protect me but instead kept Steve and God out. The weight of it crushed me. I found myself curled up on the bathroom floor more times than I could count, sobbing in a way that felt like my soul was unraveling. I couldn't meet the expectations of my husband, my children, or myself.

And then there were the darker moments when the whispers of generational curses crept in. My grandmother and mother struggled with thoughts of suicide and attempted to take their own lives. And now, it was pressing against me, telling me I was no different. I would brush my fingers across knives, imagining an escape from the unbearable pain. Can you relate to the crushing weight of a pain that never seems to end? Day after day, it lingers—the same ache, the same exhaustion, the same silent scream inside. It drains you, leaving you hollow, hopeless, and wondering if relief will ever come.

The Search for Help

I tried everything I knew—counseling, medication, prayer—but nothing seemed to touch the depths of the pain I carried. Desperate for relief, I entered an outpatient program. Sitting alone in that office, I felt like a failure. I hadn't even told Steve because I wanted to handle it on my own, as though admitting I needed help was admitting defeat and ultimate failure. However, the program began to slowly unravel the knots in my mind. I started to see patterns I had been blind to for so long. I learned that I wasn't just a victim of my past; I was a victim of my own thoughts and the lies I had come to believe. Just like Eve, I was persuaded by the accuser—a lie so close to the truth and twisted just enough to deceive me.

A Long Road to Healing

Our journey is a testament to the transformative power of faith and personal growth. It is proof that even the most fractured relationships can find new life. Two decades ago, our marriage was at a breaking point. Steve wanted to give us one last shot—a marriage conference called "Weekend to Remember." I, on the other hand, was insistent—I was done and had no hope left.

And then, God stepped in. In a moment I can only describe as divine, He allowed me to see the truth. Satan, the accuser, doesn't just whisper lies; he makes them feel like truth. He lures us into compromise, one small step at a time, until what once felt wrong becomes normal. We looked around and saw our friends making the same choices and society nodding in agreement. Suddenly, the sacred became disposable.

Everywhere we turned, the message was clear. Commercials mocked husbands, portraying them as weak, lazy, and incompetent. Women were told to show more, be more, and flaunt more because attention equaled worth. The world rewarded it, praised it, and celebrated it. And we believed the lie not in one reckless moment but through tiny, seemingly harmless choices. It was a little compromise here, a little indulgence there until we were so far in we couldn't see the way out.

Even the Bible wasn't off-limits. God gave us our bodies to enjoy, didn't He? So we twisted the truth to fit our desires. Isn't that what Satan did to Jesus and Adam and Eve, tempting them with twisted, partial truths? (The enemy knows the Bible and how to quote it to achieve his purposes.) So, we conveniently chose to forget about self-control. That part didn't feel as good. That part got left out. And with that, we abandoned restraint completely, justifying every reckless decision until the line between right and wrong was nothing more than a distant memory.

We got lost in drinking and chasing a wild life, surrounded by other adults who also had children —all finding excuses to make our choices seem acceptable. It wasn't just our decisions; it was the culture we created. It was a world where respect, honor, and reverence in marriage didn't exist; we had lost sight of each other, and love became something to use rather than protect.

We still loved each other, but looking back, we realize we didn't truly understand unconditional love. We were clinging to something that felt like love, but in reality, we were just two broken people trying to fill the emptiness inside us.

After years of walking through this mess, we weren't just battered; we were in body casts, barely holding ourselves together. We had broken each other's spirits and shattered all of our hopes. But there was something in Steve I hadn't noticed before. He wasn't just trying to change—God was changing him. At first, I doubted it. I thought it was temporary, another empty promise. But over time, I couldn't deny what I was witnessing. The man who had once been part of my pain was now being transformed before my eyes.

At the same time, something was shifting in me. I began engaging with the Bible in a way I never had before. It was no longer just a book of stories; it was alive, speaking directly to my heart. My prayers changed too. Instead of asking God to fix Steve, I asked Him to change me. It was humbling and painful, but it was the beginning of real transformation.

> "Create in me a pure heart, O God, and renew a steadfast spirit within me"
> (Psalm 51:10, NIV).

Healing wasn't instantaneous. We all want quick fixes. We grow exhausted from the fight, frustrated that things aren't fair, and overwhelmed by the journey ahead. But God doesn't ask us to have it all figured out. He simply asks us to take the next step in obedience, trusting Him with each decision and direction.

> "The Lord makes firm the steps of the one who delights in him"
> (Psalm 37:23, NIV).

Even after that pivotal moment, we still had work to do. Our home—our marriage—was still cluttered with baggage. But now, instead of tripping over it blindly, we started sorting through it. One by one, we placed the boxes in their proper rooms, deciding what could stay and what needed to go. Some things from our past were still there, tucked away, waiting for the right time. When God was ready for us to open them, we knew we could trust Him to guide us.

Healing was a process, a careful balance of moving forward while handling old wounds. It felt like walking into a room that had been rearranged. Something was different and unfamiliar. Sometimes, it felt like something was missing. Other times, new things were in place, and we had to ask, "Does this belong here?" and "Do we like it this way?" Learning how to live in a new, healthier way took time.

> "Trust in the Lord with all your heart and lean not on your own understanding;
> in all your ways submit to him, and he will make your paths straight"
> (Proverbs 3:5–6, NIV).

We also learned that tension wasn't always a sign of failure. Disagreeing was okay. Having opinions was healthy. What mattered was how we handled them. The real danger came when we walked into old rooms where boxes were still piled high, stepping through a maze of land mines and risking another explosion. But this time, we weren't as fearful. We had already cleared some space. We had learned how to breathe.

With each room we tackled, we built confidence. We could sit together without getting bruised. And as we moved into deeper areas of healing, we became more aware of ourselves, of each other, and of the process. We weren't reckless anymore. We knew what the land mines looked like, but we also knew that some might still be hidden. That didn't mean we stopped moving forward—it just meant we stepped carefully, together.

We had chosen a new way. We had chosen healing.

> "Today I have given you the choice between life and death, between blessings and curses. Now I call on heaven and earth to witness the choice you make. Oh, that you would choose life, so that you and your descendants might live!" (Deuteronomy 30:19, NLT).

The Story Unfolding

This isn't the ending of our story. It's the middle of a journey marked by God's faithfulness and redemption. The fairy tale I once dreamed of is finally coming true—but not in the way I had imagined. I love him more than ever, and he is my safe place. But I had the fairy-tale story wrong.

I left out the war.

The accuser was destined to destroy, always prowling and deceiving, whispering lies so close to the truth that I believed them. I thought love meant ease and that happily ever after came without a fight. But now I embrace the hard because I know the ending.

God is a *redeemer*—a *restorer* of what feels impossible.

I once felt one hundred percent unchangeable—too broken, too wounded. But God proved me wrong. He took what seemed irreparable and made it new. We learned not to use the d-word flippantly; divorce is not an option. That realization restored the covenant between us, the promise that we are in this through it all.

That's why we are the rib, taken from Adam, formed and made to become one. From the very beginning, Satan sowed division: Adam blamed the woman, and the woman blamed the serpent. But look at how God responded: He didn't abandon them. He loved, covered, and called them out with truth and awareness.

> *From the very beginning, Satan sowed division: Adam blamed the woman, and the woman blamed the serpent.*

We need that same truth in our marriages. What is the desire of our hearts for our covenant? Our spouse carries the same longing. But in a world filled with noise, it's hard to hear. That's why we need the armor of God in our marriages (Ephesians 6:10–17). As Priscilla Shirer teaches, it's not just about having the armor; it's about activating it through prayer, knowing what each piece means, and using it.

Our baggage doesn't feel so heavy anymore—not because it disappeared but because of our commitment to God. He has walked us through the fire. The battlefield that was our home has become a resting place.

And this? This is the love story worth fighting for.

Wounded, Weary, and Worth Fighting For: A Marriage Redemption Story

STEVE AND KESS SCHARFF

How are you showing your spouse how valuable they are through your daily actions?

What specific change are you asking God for, and how will you align your actions with His guidance to bring that transformation to life? Write down your prayer, speak it aloud, and take one step today toward living it out.

What baggage are you bringing into your marriage, and how can you take one step today toward addressing past pain before it overflows? God is a gentle healer, full of love—how can you remind yourself that healing is worth the journey?

Ask One Another

Take time to prayerfully ask one another these questions, seeking God's guidance to grow together.

Kess and Steve Scharff's ministry centers on showing the love of Jesus to everyone they meet, teaching their family to break generational sin, and teaching others to love and serve like Christ. They believe family extends beyond blood, encompassing all who love Jesus and live according to His call. Through their work with SEEDS for Change, they emphasize holistic healing, experiential growth, and breaking free from cycles of trauma by living in alignment with God's Word and being full of gratitude and joy in the simpleness of the day.

Kess and Steve have persevered through twenty-seven years of marriage, raising three beautiful daughters and a growing number of grandchildren. As a transformational coach, author, speaker, and mentor, Kess shares her journey of healing and faith. She is passionate about helping women heal from trauma, embrace their God-given purpose, and thrive in every season of life.

Steve, a business executive and devoted father, has defied worldly expectations to embrace a life of ministry. Steve's commitment to breaking generational cycles and modeling safe, loving masculinity is a testament to God's work in his life.

Through speaking and mentoring, Steve and Kess equip individuals and couples to rebuild their lives and relationships on a foundation of faith.

Their story is one of redemption, unwavering commitment, and relentless faith, where surviving in marriage means clinging to Jesus for their very next breath. They embrace God's beauty in nature, exploration, and the present moment, trusting Him through every challenge. Their marriage stands as a testament to God's transformative power, inspiring others to persevere through the hard work of love, faith, and hope.

"Therefore everyone who hears these words of mine and puts them into practice is like a wise man who built his house on the rock. The rain came down, the streams rose, and the winds blew and beat against that house; yet it did not fall, because it had its foundation on the rock. But everyone who hears these words of mine and does not put them into practice is like a foolish man who built his house on sand."

MATTHEW 7:24–26, NIV

A Marriage Built for the Storm

GARY AND TAMRA ANDRESS

Testimony Six

A Marriage Built for the Storm

By Gary and Tamra Andress

They stood on the shoreline, with hundreds of colorful umbrellas popped up amidst a summertime storm, to witness our highly anticipated "I dos." We had promised each other that "Rain or shine, we'll meet barefoot at the altar." So we did. And while our wedding party wasn't too keen on switching to boardshorts and bikinis, we viewed the day as an adventure worth sharing. Though we prayed for clear skies (halfheartedly and self-servingly), the thunder rumbled, and the lightning cracked as the crowd gasped and squealed rather than oohing and aahing over the details of the moment. The physical building of our wedding venue was even struck, and the entrance collapsed at the very moment we sealed the deal with a kiss and ran back inside to safety and dryness. With the help of a little "liquid courage," this felt freeing and idealistic, but, honestly, it was dangerous.

There are a few different sayings about rain on your wedding day. It's good luck, they say. It's a sign of fertility and lots of babies, they profess with a smile. Neither has rung true for us. Luck is fleeting, as we all know. And though we adore our precious children, we stopped shy of "lots" and gratefully parent two, our son and daughter. Rain can also be seen as renewal and cleansing in God's Word. At the time, however, we were lukewarm believers, yet to be baptized or filled with the Holy Spirit. So these words carried no weight. Any banter about renewing or cleansing wasn't even offered as a thought seed.

Several years into our marriage, lightning figuratively struck our home's foundation rather than a nearby building. This was our wake-up call: the moment we realized our "I dos" required levels of sacrifice we could hardly comprehend.

Marriage matures like we do: from children to teenagers and teenagers to adults. And just like the timing of our physical maturation, there are pivotal moments in marriage that define our health, well-being, confidence, and beliefs. We believed the exhilarating wedding ceremony would secure our lifetime love, but words fall short when actions don't align. Up until this point, we had been playing "house." The Sims simulation game that emerged in 2000 was a fair replica of our day-to-day lives. While we surely had vibrant personas and a rich connection of friendship (unlike the computer game), we hadn't explored the depths of each other's souls or the realities of each other's pasts. We were characterized by what society expected and what we thought each other wanted, needed, and loved. To be clear, most of these revelations weren't recognized or intended in the moment, but through our deep-healing journeys, we've unpacked the layers of facade, the masks we wore, and the reasons we fell into the rut of a marriage built on sand. We were immature kids playing in a very adult world—with real money, real emotions, real needs, and very real consequences.

Don't hear us wrong. We loved each other with the depth of love we witnessed growing up, glimpsed in movies, and saw glorified with "Valentine" vibes. But limited comprehension led to selfish service to one another rather than a laid-down love we would later grow into. Here are our stories:

Gary's "I Do" Story:

When you say "I do," it is based on your past experiences, what you have read, or perhaps what a mentor has shared. And expressing a sentiment that encompasses a lifetime is seemingly impossible to do in your own strength. Like the healing journey of any twelve-step recovery program, stating anything with such grandiose longevity feels stifling. *I will always be sober. I will forever or never . . .* The promise is too big for the mind to process on a human level, especially a mindset without faith. If you don't have faith, all you can rely on is hope. And hope falls short without Jesus. I didn't know what "I do" meant, but I knew I wanted her.

Three and a half years later (seven years into our relationship), I stood in front of the gym mirror, bicep curling arm by arm and staring into the helplessness of my own tired eyes. I stood processing, as I had for countless hours, a reality I had suppressed. This woman, whom I called my wife and the mother to my children, could never, in all her kindness and love, act with such disdain. She was "perfect" for me. I had created this pedestal for her, and it's where she belonged. I had essentially removed her option of free will from my mind, thinking that anything other than my idealized version couldn't possibly be true. But hunches and facts were proving me wrong. I had an avoidance mindset and had shut reality out of my mind to maintain the belief that "we are good." And my natural optimism led me to believe we could cover up this failing with the fictitious fruit of happiness.

I wasn't the only one avoiding it. We didn't communicate well about the deep, real stuff. We often had an elephant under our living room rug that we would dance around as if it didn't exist. Pains from our pasts, current problems, and even small irritabilities would be suppressed and dealt with quietly. We gloated over our argument-free relationship, mainly because we both had the natural tendency toward flight rather than fight. Our family histories led us to hide rather than face anything that could cause us pain. Plus, we had developed this "happy life" that I surely didn't want to lose, and we didn't want to project anything different. Through daily denial, we drew one step closer to the detonation of our foundation. We were both ashamed and afraid (unlike the garden, unashamed and safe), but neither of us wanted to discuss it . . . until we couldn't avoid it any longer.

> *Through daily denial, we drew one step closer to the detonation of our foundation.*

After all the details of layered unfaithfulness came to light, I witnessed this woman, whom I adored and saw as infallible, curled up in the fetal position and scared for her life. As she lay there, I recognized myself in her. I, too, had been in a fetal position metaphorically ever since my biological father abandoned me at the age of seven. He was my everything. I looked up to him. I embraced every positive memory and pushed out everything that was bad. We laughed together, played together, and adventured together. We had a real connection. And then, boom, he was gone. Abandonment led me to an avoidant attachment style that kept people at arm's length. He left me. I never wanted to feel that again, and I didn't want her to feel it either, despite the circumstances we were in. I wanted to keep her safe. I was a fixer. That's what I did (or at least thought I did until I met Jesus). I fixed broken people, even to my own detriment.

So I embraced my wife, seeing her mental fragility in that season. She wanted to take her life, and I was afraid for both my kids and myself. I would hold her in the night when she had full-body shakes. Even when I wanted to push her away the most (as she had already shattered my heart), out of fear that she could shatter our family, I kept holding on. But in the midst of becoming her protector, I pushed down my needs. I pushed down my pains and worries. And I became the rock I thought she needed, as I didn't yet understand Abba as the rock on which we stand and are secured.

Thankfully, a pastor who had been a customer years before guided us to a church in a nearby city. The Holy Spirit prompted me to send a text (before I knew the power of the Holy Spirit) asking if they had a mid-week service. I share this to say that had we not run to the feet of Jesus at the altar of that small Pentecostal-rooted church, I'm not sure we would have made it.

Grace and mercy swept over us and were exemplified through what God did for us. We started to recognize Jesus as our Lord and Savior. And I began to recognize the fail points of our humanness and the depths of the sin that encapsulated our lives. Instead of putting all my hope in her, I started putting my hope in Him, ultimately learning to forgive as He had forgiven.

I remember the moment I forgave her; it was the moment she forgave herself. I no longer harbored feelings of hopelessness, even though it was very difficult in my flesh, and I knew it was a turning point. At that very moment, she encountered Jesus in our living room (which she describes in her book about her healing journey, *Always Becoming: sex, shame and Love*), and I was able to see in both flesh and spirit someone "made new."

I still had great sadness, great confusion, and great loss, blended with layers of pain and infused with a catastrophic break of trust. Despite these feelings, I never stopped loving her, but I froze in most areas of life as I put all my energy into nurturing her. One hundred percent of my focus was on serving her so she could rebuild her self-worth. But as a result, I stopped focusing on myself. My business started falling apart, along with other relationships, and my health was shot. All I had the capacity for was to parent our toddlers and try to make sense of what happened to my marriage. As time passed and she was fully set free, I found myself back in my comfortable hiding place.

She was safe, and our family was flourishing, or so they thought. If I could just keep it that way while I picked up the other pieces of our life, I could manage it all and maintain my sanity and reputation. As you can clearly see by my repeated use of *I*, I was not releasing any of it to Jesus but instead was trying to control my way through. I fell into shame and guilt and my own destructive patterns. I had set up our life on a high-risk, fragile foundation, and it was taking all I had to keep it from crashing to the ground. And though God was in the midst, I had my hands clenched tightly around the steering wheel of my life.

We live in a me-centric society. Often, our love can be self-serving and filled with selfish desires and tendencies. From that perspective, we look to get something from our spouse and find ourselves asking, "If we serve them, how will it best serve our needs and our house? How will it serve to keep the peace and exchange value." I don't believe any of this is done maliciously; I certainly didn't have a hurtful intent, but any false idol we serve, we serve selfishly. Even as a married couple works together with a "we-centric" plan, there is still a lack of emphasis on the family of God, and they can remove God as the center point. I tried to keep the focus on her happiness and told myself I was doing it for my family, but I was actually serving myself all along. The more effort I put into covering up the mess I had made and the shameful points of my life (in the guise of serving her), the bigger the mess became. I was once again avoiding the truths of the situation. And I was omitting truths, not letting her into the parts of me that needed mending. The more I lied, the more I was bound to my secrets.

Avoiding something will always result in a consequence. If we don't expose the traumas of our everyday lives, we risk accumulating decades' worth of unresolved pain and sorrow. It's much easier to process the highs and lows of a moment than the highs and lows of a lifetime. Checking in and accountability are absolutely vital to the success of a marriage. I now know (even though it took me nearly a decade to expose all I was harboring inside and lying to protect) that being proactive in communicating needs, desires, realities, and the stories we tell ourselves is paramount to starting and maintaining the healing process. This is loving sacrificially versus idolizing someone. When I say "I do" now, similar to the sobriety or addiction process, I am saying "I do" to the day. It is a one-day-at-a-time mindset. And now, instead of having hope in our marriage, I have a firm-rooted faith in Christ, which gives me confidence. Our life on Earth is such a short period of time when compared to our eternity in heaven. We have the Father's love that is unwavering; it's not an idol that can fall. I can trust in Him and the Holy Spirit in her and me, and therefore, I can trust in us. Every idol I've ever worshiped in the flesh has fallen into ruin because it was not built on a foundation of rock. Idols (like money, lust, notoriety, and physicality) have no value. The Rock keeps me secure in our marriage, and my value is found only in Him.

> *Avoiding something will always result in a consequence.*
> *If we don't expose the traumas of our everyday lives,*
> *we risk accumulating decades' worth of unresolved pain and sorrow.*

Sacrificial love is a love that has Jesus infused within it. It's not idolized love. It's not selfish. It is instead a third-cord love, a strong love that's ever-strengthening. When a cord is placed under tension, it eventually reaches a breaking point, but a three-cord strand is strong enough to hold that pressure. And God sent Jesus for this kind of love. The sacrificing aspect of this love is to die to your flesh so that you don't lead with your infallible self. Instead, you bring a living love to your marriage and a willingness to face the hard together, imperfectly alongside the perfect One. Transparent conversations that expose our weaknesses will strengthen us as a collective. When we lay it all down at the feet of Jesus, He has a perfect will and game plan. And we are looking for His will, not ours. Ultimately, the desires of our hearts become His, and we are given the gift of embracing lively, spirit-birthed fruit from abiding, not hiding. I'm no longer abandoned; I've been adopted. And together, we are one in Him.

Tamra's "I Do" Story:

I used to jokingly share that I had a quarter-life crisis so that I didn't have to have a midlife one. You got a sneak peek into that time by reading Gary's vantage point.

The silly, repeated commentary was one of those "no, but really" types of statements. I was certain I had rebuilt our marriage, brick by brick, alongside the Father. Even as I write this, I see myself geared up in my Rosie-the-Riveter outfit with arm guns out, red polka-dot hair wrap in place, and a sold-out intention to heal, build, and embrace all the promises that a healthy, rock-solid marriage would have. I see Jesus alongside me with His bricks and mortar and tool belt. But I don't see Gary, which obviously became the problem I was blissfully unaware of.

After I got my feet firmly planted *post–rock bottom*, as some would say (I say *post–rock foundation*), I was ready to move into a growth zone. And Gary was lovingly providing all of the support I needed financially, energetically, and relationally (or so I believed). For three years, I focused inward toward the nucleus of our home while also confronting the depths of my soul's weariness and the root concerns that had led me down this dark path of hiddenness and isolation. I participated in a year-long worship school and biweekly therapy sessions for our marriage and for myself. Later, I entered a two-year leadership multiplication institute program in our church and was ordained as a certified minister. My new passion and pursuit of Jesus felt freeing, life-giving, holistic, and healthy in mind, body, soul, and spirit. I had a fresh wind and what truly felt like a second chance at life.

And yet, that focus on self-development, even if well-intentioned, had me hyperfocused on all things new, allowing no room to notice the red flags flying around me. When I finally noticed that things seemed awry, it was too late. Unfortunately, due to the enemy's tactics of cycling shame and my avoidance tendencies toward conflict, I chose to mostly ignore what was going on in my marriage. Taking the blame on myself because of my previous fault points, I let Gary's missteps go without the same excavation process. *It was my fault, after all*, or so I was led to believe, both in my own story patterns and through his projected pain.

You're probably aware that when two people say "I do," they are saying "I do" to their pasts, not just their futures. But there is another layer to consider when two people (unhealed and far from Jesus) come together in their brokenness. They often approach their relationship with a hopelessly-in-love mentality and the assumption that the affection of the other will heal all wounds as they ride off into the sunset together as one. The very opposite is true. If I could have depicted our wedding day (beyond the beach scene) in the spirit realm, you would have seen both of us lugging generational ties, sexual traumas, perverted beliefs of love and intimacy, bondage from other careless relationships, and a slew of idols we kept shelved in the crevices of our hearts.

You have probably heard the phrase "Love is blind." Well, over the next several years (even after the painful experience I suppressed and kept secret in order to maintain his reputation and honor his less public, less vocal way of dealing with things), the cycles of shadows continued without my knowledge. I watched him repent, but this time, it was my turn to forgive. We got baptized again together and even had another proposal, later remarrying with this revived love. I remember trying on the wedding dresses after having my purity in Christ restored and discovering a level of intimacy with my husband that I never knew I needed. That day, I felt giddy in a new way, a matured way. And though I had experienced a throne-room wedding with the King of Kings years earlier, this felt like an overflow moment of abundance as I embraced the joy of celebrating and sealing our love with just our kids—an intimate moment on the same sandy shores.

This time, it wasn't quite the same storm, but there was rain and wind that tried to stop it from happening. Ultimately, the sunbursts claimed the evening's sunset, and the thunder and lightning rolled in the distance beyond Gary's head as we exchanged vows. I just knew this "I do" was it. I thought how perfect it was that God would give us a reminder of the past and a glimpse of the sunny future. We danced on the shoreline and in the waves with our kiddos and grabbed the sunflares with our kisses. This was what I wanted for every woman, man, and family. But now, when I see those pictures hanging in my house, parts of my soul break, knowing my reality wasn't the full picture and the storm was still looming, unseen, and hidden. You see, even when light is present, one can still hide if they are determined to stay in the shadows that have become their protective barriers, their sense of safety. And unfortunately, it can be under the guise of protecting, providing, and nurturing.

Everything in a relationship requires personal reflection and ownership because pointing fingers leaves three fingers pointing back at you. After my second wedding, the Lord was gracious in pressing me in the development of my gift of discernment. I wasn't "praying without ceasing" for my marriage because I thought we were good, so I took my eyes off the prize of covenant love and focused on other things. At times, I even found myself questioning my own intentions, seeking support from the Lord in areas He was pressing on my heart (like money), not yet knowing they were being pressed for Gary's sake. I was oblivious to the catastrophe that had been building. I thought he was incapable of something other than the idealized role he had played, a role similar to the one he had conjured up about me the decade before. As much as I loved Jesus and lived my life surrendered to Him, I also trusted Gary as my protector and provider. And while I knew those roles were ultimately held by Abba, the comforts and consistency being bought, presented, and depicted had become my daily safety and norm. Gary had developed a lifestyle for us that became impossible for him to maintain as the snowball he had created became an avalanche.

Idolization and *infidelity* are words that make most people want to run. And biblically, they give an out to this contract. But God never released me. He helped me stay. He helped me find the pockets of sunshine prepared for me in advance so that in my weakness, and despite my body's desire to run and find safety, He would be glorified. I never questioned if Gary loved me; I questioned if he really loved God. But regardless, I knew his understanding of love was juvenile and stifled. I idolized him. I leaned into him as my earthly knight in shining armor during my trauma healing, and he had become so good at fixing everything that I misread every stressor as heroic and every misstep as happenstance. I idolized a false reality because that's what was presented as truth.

All the building Jesus and I had done on that foundation felt completely destroyed and reduced to rubble. Standing amidst the destruction, I wondered what my reality was. Who is this man I married? Do I even know him? I slept next to him every night, and he seemed at peace. His stories and tales, though larger than life, seemed true. But after dissection and lots of processing, there were hooks uncovered that had not yet released him from his own childhood: bad habits, destructive beliefs, weaknesses that he wouldn't admit to, and strengths that were simply defense mechanisms arising from his own efforts and not from God's intended covering or help.

The pressures men feel as the caretakers of our homes can be insurmountable and often silent, but in a healthy home and a marriage based on communion, there is safety to share and grace in asking for help. None of us are meant to carry the weight alone. And when we yolk ourselves to burdens instead of delighting in Christ and relishing in His ability, we will silently run ourselves into the grave. And every night, we'll fall asleep not in peace but in utter exhaustion from doing life in our own strengths and insufficiencies.

What do I do now? I learned from the isolated pain of the last breakdown that I would not bear the weight of this burden by myself. I learned that keeping it silent would keep me from the gifts and encouragement God had given me in our church family. I learned that my false sense of security and provision from man was hindering my relationship with Christ. I learned that having faith in God to prosper me while relying on earthly treasures was a halfhearted devotion. I learned that stuffing my emotions, even from God, would put me back in the bondage of the masks I worked so hard to eliminate.

So I cried. And I shared sacred moments with sisters and brothers in Christ. And I ran to the feet of Jesus with every tear, every burst of anger, every question. It was truly a Job season—pressed and tested from every angle. And I became content with being discontent in circumstances yet fully content in Yahweh—the very one who breathed into me life, hope, and even joy in the midst of darkness.

I've heard it said this way by Pastor Bianca Olthoff: "Secrecy is sin, while privacy is protection." I will protect the details of my husband's pain and consequences, but I will not keep them a secret for his sake or for mine. Instead, we will stand and shout of the goodness of God that chases us down daily to remind us of His great sufficiency and the ultimate sacrifice that displayed the greatest love we've ever known. The love that has the ultimate staying power. The love that covers a multitude of sins. The love that penetrated the hearts of our children as they bore witness to the pains of the problems and still remained trusting and loving. The same love that allowed us to separate for a time to tend to our souls and reunited us to confirm our future as secure in Him. Even on the days when running and hiding would have been easier, this love pushed us into one another—because *this* love is patient and kind. "It does not envy, it does not boast, it is not proud. It does not dishonor others, it is not self-seeking, it is not easily angered, it keeps no record of wrongs. Love does not delight in evil but rejoices with the truth. It always protects, always trusts, always hopes, always perseveres" (1 Corinthians 13:4–7, NIV).

> *I've heard it said this way by Pastor Bianca Olthoff:*
> *"Secrecy is sin, while privacy is protection."*

And though we may have been married on sandy shores, there is no other explanation for our continued commitment to one another than the rock Himself. And our mustard seed of faith kept us secure. What lies ahead for our marriage is unknown to us, but we stand united, pushing back the gates of Hades and proclaiming the name of Jesus over every new structure He is building on this firm foundation. And even though we don't know the whole story yet, we are confident and thankful for the victory of today . . . because love never fails. Even when trust is shattered, love will hold on. Upon the recommitment of Gary's life to the Lord, we began working as one to emulate Christ's character traits, habits, patterns, and tendencies—first through daily surrender and then through daily forgiveness. We will die to ourselves so that we may live in Him alone.

Most people will write from their mountaintop, but God is calling us to shout out to those who are in the valley of the shadow of death. Fear no evil, for His rod and His staff will comfort you. You are not alone (Psalm 23:4). And your idea of love pales in comparison to His display of love on the cross. He came for you and me. His body was broken, and His blood was shed for this very reason. And marriage is an expression of His heart for His church—broken in our sin but rebuilt and made whole in His gift of salvation. And though, for now, we imperfectly pursue wholeness daily, one day, there will be the most glorious wedding, with the most radiant light penetrating any attempt at darkness or storm . . . because perfect love casts out all fear.

And so we are here, inviting you into the cool of the day, naked and unafraid. Still saying "I do," but first to Jesus.

I do, and I will. Because He did, and He does.

A Marriage Built for the Storm
GARY AND TAMRA ANDRESS

Ask Him: What areas have you hidden away from your bride in an effort to protect her or you? Consider past traumas, current pressures, or future fears.

Ask Her: Where have you created self-preserving blind spots in your marriage in order to stay comfortable or avoid the hard conversations, moves, or expectations of what is required beyond complacency?

Ask Yourself: Have I created a false idol of my spouse? Where am I guilty of infidelity: relationally, emotionally, financially, spiritually?

Ask One Another
Take time to prayerfully ask one another these questions, seeking God's guidance to grow together.

Gary and Tamra Andress have shared seventeen years together, thirteen of those as husband and wife. Raised by the ocean, they're lifelong beach lovers, raising two wave-chasing children of their own. Navigating the complexities of a dual-entrepreneur household has brought challenges and abundant blessings.

Once focused on worldly success and comfort, their lives were radically transformed in 2016 when they surrendered their hearts to Jesus at the altar. Since then, their faith has been the foundation of their relationships, businesses, and life's purpose. Tamra's ordination in 2019 deepened her commitment to God's call, further equipping her to say yes to His will. Both have encountered the profound love of Jesus in various seasons and cherish every baptism they've witnessed—especially those of their children and family—as beautiful reminders of His enduring grace and mercy.

This project marks their first written collaboration, with Tamra capturing Gary's insights through heartfelt Q&A sessions. United in their calling, they feel led to minister to marriages, families, and the marketplace. While they currently host transformative wholeness retreats individually for men and women, they are preparing to offer future retreats tailored to couples and families.

Their non-profit, The Founder Collective, is a platform for sharing their testimony and empowering marketplace ministers through weekly virtual discipleship, an annual conference, and The Founder Academy, set to launch in 2027.

V.I.C.T.O.R.Y. Marriage
A Blueprint for Lasting Love Curriculum for Married Couples

Testimonies will stand the test of time, just as they did from the Old Testament to the New Testament. It's why storytelling is so significant and deep-seated in our cultural practices, entertainment, and family traditions for creating lasting memories and generational impact. However, we may lose sight of how the "happily ever after" ending transpired from a granular state, requiring us to question how they got from point A to point B. Even with the miraculous redemption of Christ's intercession to make us new, He, too, is a process God. In the following pages, you will read Tamra and Gary's process for ultimately winning the battle against the enemy when he's hard-pressed to cause division in a marriage.

From communication and financial stressors to intimacy issues, parental differences, trust and betrayal, addictions, and beyond . . . this process was cultivated through years of therapy, seeking Jesus, and mentorship. Our prayer is that you implement these practical applications, present them to the Lord, and prepare your hearts for remaking, reshaping, and recommitting to your covenant love.

Victory Is Submission
"Submit yourselves, then, to God. Resist the devil, and he will flee from you" (James 4:7, NIV). *"Submit to one another out of reverence for Christ"* (Ephesians 5:21, NIV).

Marriage is a journey of submission—first to Christ and then to one another. Through practical exercises and deep heart work, this framework equips couples to walk in unity, sacrifice, and biblical love.

"V" is for Volley
The Art of Questioning & Sharing Responsibilities

Key Scripture: *"Let each of you look not only to his own interests, but also to the interests of others" (Philippians 2:4, ESV).*

Marriage is a constant exchange of energy, responsibilities, love, and leadership. Just as Jesus answered with questions, we must volley conversation and responsibility in seasons of change.

Discussion & Exercises: Practice active listening, storytelling, vulnerable sharing, and heart reflection.

Communication Activity! For fun, try answering questions with a question (Qw/Q). Christ did this throughout the Scriptures to help the listener engage in their own thought processes, perspectives, and patterns.

- **Biblical Example: Authority of Jesus Questioned - Matt 21:23–27**
  Chief priests ask: *"By what authority are You doing these things?"*
  Jesus responds: *"Was John's baptism from heaven or from men?"*
  He turns the trap back on them, exposing their fear of man.

- **Biblical Example: The Good Samaritan - Luke 10:25–37**
  Lawyer asks: "Who is my neighbor?"
  Jesus responds: "Which of these three do you think was a neighbor?"
  He shifts the focus from who qualifies as a neighbor to how to be a neighbor.

The convo continues... Do you see how this de-escalated what could have become an argument?

"V" is for Volley
Continued...

- **Marital Example:** Sarah feels overwhelmed by household responsibilities while juggling work. Jason is unaware of her needs and pressures, so instead of being defensive, he uses Jesus's Qw/Q approach.

Sarah: Why do I always have to be the one managing everything at home? Don't you see how exhausted I am?

Jason: That sounds really hard. I had no idea. What part feels the heaviest for you right now?

Sarah: Everything! Work, kids, home . . . I can't breathe and have no time to myself; meanwhile, you get Sunday football and sleep in while I clean on Saturdays.

Jason: I hadn't thought of it like that. I thought you enjoyed that time What's something I can take off your plate?

Sarah: Groceries, cooking, and kitchen cleanup a couple of times a week would be great so I don't have to rush home every day and can actually enjoy eating with you and the kids.

Jason: With the kids' sports schedules, are there certain days that would work best for you?

Warning: Don't let this become a bad habit or an area of tension in your marriage. Instead, make it a playful activity that supports honesty and gives healthy space for processing rather than probing or interrogating. The more questions, the more opportunity you have to get to the root cause and the heart behind the original question, which may stem from a place of friction.

"V" is for Volley
Continued...

Why This Works: Instead of being defensive, asking questions can lead to clarity. Rather than resolving a problem too quickly for the sake of a temporary peace, it is beneficial for your spouse to process the depths of their emotions. This approach will allow you to arrive at a unified solution together. Instead of assuming what the other needs, honor one another and allow them to voice their concerns. This practice also makes room for leading spiritually rather than mentally or emotionally, which instills peace instead of chaos. Ultimately, this turns conflict into connection. YOUR TURN.

Check-In Questions:

"What can I do for you today (or this week or in this season)?"
This is a pivotal practice of loving others as yourself. We often wake up in the morning selfishly focused on our day, our needs, and our priorities. This selfless act and moment of consideration will take you out of your own head and allow you to be on one team and in one accord, serving one another as Christ serves us.

"What is your energy level this week?"
Checking in with your spouse about their health (mind, body, and spirit) enables you to better balance the load, care for each other's needs, and, most importantly, gain insight on how to pray specifically for them in real-time.

"How can we refuel together?" Moving your schedule from me to we—we say MWE (reference from Tamra's solo publication Always Becoming; sex, shame and Love, where you can learn more intimate details of their marriage journey). Self-care practices have become all the rage, but they sometimes isolate us from one another. And while we are huge advocates of solo intimacy with Christ, spending dedicated play and rest time together creates momentum for the heavier, less connected days.

Reflection: Needs shift based on seasons. Sometimes, seasons shift abruptly, and these crucial discussions get missed, causing friction. So how do we adapt when seasons shift unexpectedly?

"V" is for Volley
Continued...

PRAYER COVERING FOR VOLLEY

Lord, we come to you with surrendered hearts and minds. We ask that you help us manage our emotions, rewire our offended spirits, and be ever aware of your presence in the midst of our conversations. We humbly come as servants not only to you but to one another. Make us keenly aware of one another's needs, desires, hopes, and dreams so that we can walk in one accord in the divine plan you have for our marriage. God, help me rise to the occasion of love and give me eyes to see my spouse in every season. Make known to me how best to pursue them as you pursue me. I exchange my selfishness with your generosity and my need to be right with your sovereign ways. My time and treasures are gifts from you; may you multiply them to be shared in overflow while also giving me a passion for loving my wife/husband as you do. Purely. Wholly. And Daily.
In Jesus name, Amen.

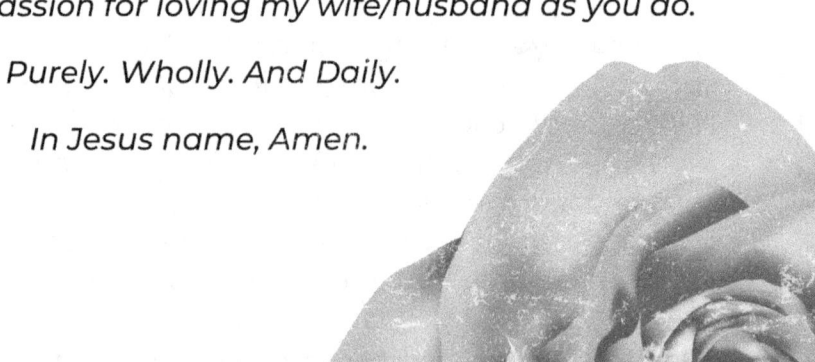

"I" is for Intimacy
and eye contact: Lights- On Love!

Key Scripture: *"That is why a man leaves his father and mother and is united to his wife, and they become one flesh" (Genesis 2:24, NIV).*

This verse establishes God's design for marriage and physical intimacy as a union of two becoming one. Intimacy is more than physical; it's emotional, spiritual, and relational.

True connection requires presence (devices down) and security (cheek-to-cheek closeness.

Discussion & Exercises: Eye Contact Exercise

Look into your spouse's eyes and name all the colors you see.

- This simple yet profound exercise will allow you to embrace the beauty that is your spouse and the intimate way they were created by the maker. God has placed exquisite attention on just their eye color; imagine how much more emphasis He has placed on their entirety.
- An added measure of presence is needed with this activity: light music, patience, timing, and sacred silence as you take them in and share with them things they may never have noticed about themselves. Give their eye color its own name: sunflower explosion (hazel/brown), ocean air (blues and grays).

"I" is for Intimacy
continued...

Honesty in Marriage: Addressing the "little white lies" that create distance. Think of this activity as accountability rather than pointing fingers or calling out. This will allow exaggerated expressions to be tamed and accuracy and humility to be exchanged.

- **Intimacy requires rigorous honesty and safety:**
  - "What would make you feel safe when we have conversations so you can share every detail instead of holding back elements you think will frustrate or hurt me?"
  - "What situations have you encountered recently that made you feel the need to extend the truth to protect yourself?" (Consider past relationships, shared seasons as a couple, childhood experiences, current situations, or areas of tension.)

- **Recall stories you've shared from your past:**
  - "When have you only told me a fraction of the whole truth?"
  - "In terms of safety, are there any areas you want to expand on so you can be fully seen and we can continue to build on a firm foundation?"

REMEMBER...

We can protect one another only when we are on one accord. Privacy is meant for the public (anyone outside of the marriage bed). Secrets will starve intimacy.

"I" is for Intimacy
continued...

"Are there any areas of secrecy from your past or present that you can entrust to me as your partner for accountability in order to restore intimacy?"

"Secrets are sin, privacy is protection." Pastor Bianca Olthoff

"Have there been areas of weight that you've opted not to share with me in order to protect me from pain, worry, or doubt in you (e.g., relationship, finances, parenting, character, etc.)?

- Take this intimacy into your bedroom: Talk can amplify your experience of love and allow you to find new levels of enjoyment as one.
- Proverbs 12:22 (NIV): "The Lord detests lying lips, but he delights in people who are trustworthy."

Redeeming Lost Places:

How can we reclaim broken moments and turn them into sacred memories? This activity can be a real thrill. It asks you to revisit old locations, vacations, and experiences with new vibrancy and hope that allows for redemption instead of tainted recounts.

Set your agenda to redeem lost locations:
- Go back to the location of your first date.
- Take that trip again to the same destination.

"I" is for Intimacy
continued...

PRAYER COVERING FOR INTIMACY

Father, I repent for hiding behind white lies because of implanted fear, worry, doubt, and even complacency in sin. I ask that you search my heart and make it pure. Reestablish trust and openness in my mind and a new desire for intimate communication with my spouse. Reinstate purity in and through me and my marriage so that we may fully encounter the beauty of love that you promised us in covenant love. Make me brave enough to reveal the areas of bondage that I've held in secrecy from my spouse. Cover me with your cloak of righteousness and bring me peace that transcends understanding. Allow us to see one another as you see us, without shame or condemnation and in truth and light. You are my Lord and Savior, and I trust you will work all things together for my good. I don't want to hide anymore. Freedom exists in you. Thank you for your grace. Amen.

"C" is for Calling
Individual Gifts, Collective Fruit & Marital Mission

Key Scripture: *We have different gifts, according to the grace given to each of us" (Romans 12:6, NIV).*

Marriage isn't just about love—it's about legacy. God designed each spouse with a unique purpose, yet their gifts must harmonize for kingdom impact.

Discussion & Exercises: Identify your spiritual gifts. *(Personal Reflection)*

Romans 12:6–8 (NIV): Gifts of Grace
"We have different gifts, according to the grace given to each of us. If your gift is prophesying, then prophesy in accordance with your faith; if it is serving, then serve; if it is teaching, then teach; if it is to encourage, then give encouragement; if it is giving, then give generously; if it is to lead, do it diligently; if it is to show mercy, do it cheerfully."

1 Corinthians 12:4–11 (NIV): Variety of Spiritual Gifts
"There are different kinds of gifts, but the same Spirit distributes them. . . . To one there is given through the Spirit a message of wisdom, to another a message of knowledge by means of the same Spirit, to another faith by the same Spirit, to another gifts of healing by that one Spirit, to another miraculous powers, to another prophecy, to another distinguishing between spirits, to another speaking in different kinds of tongues, and to still another the interpretation of tongues. All these are the work of the same Spirit, and he distributes them to each one, just as he determines."

"C" is for Calling
continued...

Ephesians 4:11–13 (NIV): Leadership Gifts in the Church
"So Christ himself gave the apostles, the prophets, the evangelists, the pastors and teachers, to equip his people for works of service, so that the body of Christ may be built up until we all reach unity in the faith and in the knowledge of the Son of God and become mature, attaining to the whole measure of the fullness of Christ."

Activity: The Fruit of the Spirit

Galatians 5:22–23 (NIV): "But the fruit of the Spirit is love, joy, peace, forbearance [patience], kindness, goodness, faithfulness, gentleness and self-control. Against such things there is no law."

After reading Galatians 5:22–23, **identify your lowest-hanging fruit** (those you possess in abundance) to give bountifully. Be sure to identify those you'd like to cultivate further as well.

See if your spouse can identify them and create a means to share and grow together. Sharing with your spouse may look like the following: "This is how, in my abiding, I seek joy. . . Let's pursue this together through prayer and play."

"C" is for Calling
continued...

Couples Reflection:

Identify how your spouse serves best and how you can honor their strengths. This is beyond the love language (Gary Chapman's book). Go deeper into your uniquely designed makeup and learn the synergy points to flourish as one.

Marital Mission Statement:

Define a shared calling and commitment as a couple. This activation helps you to remain on one accord. Use this as a gauge to decipher whether you should choose to embrace something new together or let go of something old. Conflict should be addressed while coming together for a mutually beneficial kingdom solution.

- Eyes up and devices down.
- Engage in cheek-to-cheek security—literally. Hold each other's faces to embrace closeness, tears, tension, and surrender.
- Keep hard conversations out of the bedroom. Find another sacred space to communicate so that the bedroom becomes a space of redemption and safety for both of you.
- Make the "Couple's Reflection" and the "Marital Mission Statement" a date-night convo.

"C" is for Calling
continued...

PRAYER COVERING FOR CALLING

Heavenly Father, we understand that trying to set our own path, rather than calling your kingdom come and your will be done, can be futile for our marriage. We ask that as you order our steps, you make your path known to us as we travail the roads ahead together. Keep us in tandem with your will for our lives and give us divine wisdom and clarity regarding the ultimate purpose of our marriage through our calling and kingdom service to one another and to your church. Help us to hold our tongues and deposit your Word into our hearts so that we may speak life over and to our spouse. Reveal to us the gifts you have intentionally placed in our partner and how, together, our gifts represent you and your all-encompassing character of love. We are so grateful that you have brought us together as one to emulate you on the earth. Help us to be better stewards of our blessings, namely each other, so that we can walk in humility with others and example your forgiveness through Christ. Thank you for the fresh outpouring over us so we may experience the rich, bountiful fruit of abiding in you. We love you.

In Jesus's majestic,
matchless name, Amen.

"T" is for Time-In:
Healing, Therapy & Communication

Key Scripture: *"The Lord is close to the brokenhearted and saves those who are crushed in spirit" (Psalm 34:18, NIV).*

The world teaches time-out—avoidance, withdrawal—but true healing comes from time-in. This is where we confront wounds, understand triggers, and build lasting intimacy.

Discussion & Exercises: Marital Health Assessment (Scale 1–10). Scale each question below and calculate the sum to find the average. Then, set a goal for growth.

Calculate and then set your growth goal!

SCORE   GOAL

_____   1. Do we pray together?

_____   2. How well do we feel understood by one another?

_____   3. Are we comfortable sharing our fears, struggles, and dreams without fear of judgment?

_____   4. Do we work through disagreements with grace & respect?

_____   5. Do we prioritize physical touch, affection, and intimacy in ways that meet both of our needs?

_____   6. Do we prioritize quality time or feel more like roommates?

_____   7. How well do we practice forgiveness? (Do we hold onto resentment or past mistakes?)

_____   8. Do we set marital goals and dream of the future together?

"T" is for Time-In
continued...

Questions to Ponder:

Where are we strong?
Where do we need healing?

Family Upbringing Reflection:

What generational patterns are influencing your marriage? This activity is designed to encourage self-examination of your parents' engagement in their marriage through the lens of your childhood. It also aims to ensure that new parental strategies are being established that will inhibit old habits from becoming normalized routines

Warning: If you carry offense into this activity, it can create a fence between the two of you

Areas to consider include conversation styles, roles and expectations of wife vs. husband, PDA (personal displays of affection) habits, and accountability. Also, consider your lens on therapy. Are you pro or con?

"T" is for Time-In
continued...

Therapy & Mediation:

Why is outside counsel (spiritual or professional) crucial?

- Wise counsel brings clarity and perspective while providing an objective lens to work toward resolution. It can also help bridge the gap of pain for ultimate forgiveness and reconciliation.

> "WHERE THERE IS NO GUIDANCE, A PEOPLE FALLS, BUT IN AN ABUNDANCE OF COUNSELORS THERE IS SAFETY." PROVERBS 11:14 (ESV)

- Who is cheering you toward one another? Identify mentors, spiritual leaders, coaches/therapists, or healthy-couple friendships. This is a critical element of accountability, and it can reveal where you are predominantly spending your time. We want our circle to be speaking life over our marriage, not death.

LIST THE NAMES OF PEOPLE/ ORGANIZATIONS HERE

"T" is for Time-In
continued...

PRAYER COVERING FOR TIME-IN

Jesus, you are the author and the finisher of our faith. Time to you is but a vapor, and yet, you never waste a moment. As we pour into our marriage with intentionality and focus on your perfect will to manifest through us as one, we ask that you bless us with patience, kindness, gentleness, and love for one another. We know we are fallible. We know we fall short. May your strength be perfected in our weaknesses. May we never be too proud to ask for help. May you surround us with godly marriages, mentors, and ministries that will pour into us and call us higher. May we not run away in shame from one another but instead run to you for the healing balm that only you can provide. Our past does not define us, and we pray that our identity rests in you alone so that through our testimony, you may be all the more glorified. We thank you that we have been adopted as your son and daughter into a family of love, great satisfaction, and freedom. Please forgive us for partaking in the ways of the world in our marriage and our home. Right our hearts. Fix our eyes on you, the Holy One.
And keep us protected from the enemy's tactics
of division. We seek unity through you, God.
In your wonderful name, Amen

"O" is for Ordinary
Finding the Extraordinary in the Mundane

Key Scripture: *"Do not despise these small beginnings, for the Lord rejoices to see the work begin" (Zechariah 4:10, NLT).*

Marriage isn't always adrenaline-filled. Ordinary days require intentionality and dedication to keep the connection alive. This one may seem lighthearted and simplistic, but sometimes, that's exactly what the Father calls for—childlike play and wonder. Don't take yourself too seriously. It gets to be fun.

In a society that grooms high achievers for their careers, we aren't taught to do the same for our marriages. How can you set yourself up for success in ordinary seasons when it feels like you're two ships that pass in the night?

Discussion & Exercises: Your Love Quotient: People have an IQ & an EQ (emotional intelligence). Let's find out what your LQ is by answering the questions below:

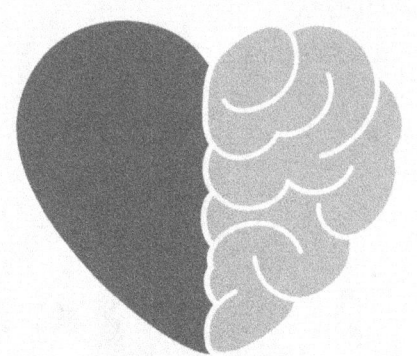

- Define what love is to you in THIS season. This definition will change based on need, desire, maturity, etc.
- Rank yourself 1–100 on where you fall within this definition.
- Listen to your spouse's definition and rank yourself on their LQ.
- Compare without judgment and discuss areas of growth.

"O" is for Ordinary
Finding the Extraordinary in the Mundane

The Tuesday & Turks Principle: How do we cultivate excitement, even in our day-to-day?

- Imagine Turks and Caicos—a honeymoon-type adventure. Now jump to a typical Tuesday. How can you infuse Turks into Tuesday?

- Come up with ideas together. Schedule them into your weeks, even if they are just five minutes of fun, like a text reminder of that beachside daydreaming, a photo share of anticipation for an adventure to come, a date night, etc.

Adventure Inventory: List fun, shared activities that keep your marriage exciting. It's not an end-of-life bucket list; it's a daily-life consistent list!

Stack Play: Tickle fights, dance-offs, question card games—how do you infuse joy into the mundane? This is how you extract EXTRA-ordinary from ordinary days.

"O" is for Ordinary
continued...

PRAYER COVERING FOR ORDINARY

Oh God, we come to you seeking joy and lightheartedness. We want to exchange our heavy-laden burdens of life with your light yoke. We know we have allowed societal mechanisms and routines to rip us from your rich ways of dwelling and being. We've become robotic in our relationships and even our time with you, Lord. We desire an extraordinary life that represents your magnificence, beauty, and wonder. Will you reinstill childlike playfulness in our eagerness to be with you and with our spouse? We know love isn't butterflies, but you have a way of breathing new life into old areas that have collected dust or been cocooned for far too long. Bless us in this season as we yearn for our marriage to be revived and restored to the passion of those early dating days. Help us to recall the things we loved most about one another and fan our flame of passion and adventure. We don't want to be complacent in our marriage. We want to experience new levels of joy and excitement. We want to lean into our love rather than run and hide or suppress and ignore. Tighten us as one —as you are the third cord that keeps us united. Thank you for your jovial, zesty nature that keeps life exciting and fruitful. Reveal this to us in our day-to-day. We love you, Amen.

"R" is for Recipe
Ingredients of a Healthy Marriage

Key Scripture: *"But the fruit of the Spirit is love, joy, peace, patience, kindness, goodness, faithfulness, gentleness, [and] self-control" (Galatians 5:22–23, ESV).*

Marriage is a blend of ingredients—some sweet, some bitter. The right balance creates a flavorful, lasting covenant.

Discussion & Exercises: The Heart Ingredients Inventory

- As you analyze the ingredients of your life, what's consuming the intended flavor?
- What's taking away from the flavor of other things?
- What's causing it to rise too much or fall flat?
    - Humility vs. Pride
    - Contentment vs. Envy
    - Intimacy vs. Lust
    - Gratitude vs. Greed
    - Peace vs. Wrath

ADD YOUR OWN LIST

"R" is for Recipe
Ingredients of a Healthy Marriage

More Marriage Ingredients:

- A thriving, God-fearing marriage requires the right balance of ingredients, many of which are forgotten, overlooked, or never taught. This list is not exhaustive. Feel free to insert your own ingredients.
  - Pray together daily.
  - Study Scripture as a couple—process together and apply together.
  - Make decisions with biblical wisdom.
  - Prioritize acts of love.
  - Practice grace over grudge.
  - Express needs, fears, and desires with vulnerability.
  - Keep your word—even small promises build long-term trust.
  - Apologize quickly.
  - Preserve undistracted time together.
  - Keep your romance alive.
  - Honor physical intimacy.
  - Stand firm.
  - Refuse to entertain escape routes.
  - Fight for each other, not against.
  - Remember inside jokes.
  - Support each other's dreams.
  - Serve together.
  - Retain wise mentorship.
  - Maintain healthy Christian friendships.

"R" is for Recipe
continued...

Forgiveness & Grace: Are we quick to forgive or slow to let go?

- The Word tells us to forgive 7 x 70. It isn't about keeping track or counting the number; it's about forgiving more times than you could ever count, as that's how many times you've been forgiven.
- Often, the one we need to forgive most is ourselves. Share with one another vulnerable areas where you'd like to forgive yourself (even if they don't have to do with your spouse). Don't make it about the other person; instead, share the intimate thoughts and ponderings of your heart and mind.

Friendship: Oftentimes, we are so focused on the formalized idea of "being married" that we forget the very valid portion of our relationship that catalyzed it to begin with. Hopefully, the last letter we unpacked, "O" ordinary, kicked this concept off, but sometimes, even adventure can distract from the heart of friendship. Jesus is our friend as much as He is our father, teacher, healer, and redeemer.

We've focused on forgiveness. Now let's focus on friendship. There has never been a truer "BFF" than the one God gifted you through your spouse.
In what ways can you be a better friend to your spouse?
- *Check in on them.*
- *Surprise them.*
- *Send them a word of encouragement.*
- *Speak life into something they may deem insignificant.*
- *Share reasons you are thankful for them.*

"R" is for Recipe
continued...

PRAYER COVERING FOR RECIPE

Oh, wonderful Creator. You are the artist, the chef, the designer of our very nature. Your creativity inspires us from the moment we open our eyes in the morning to the last breath we recall before we slip into slumber. The recipe of life is beyond what our minds can even comprehend. Your ways are higher, and your thoughts are higher. And you did not and do not miss a thing. We surrender our ideas of a perfect marriage to you, for you are the inventor of the bride and the bridegroom. Your passion is relationships. Your very triune nature is a representation of this truth. Will you be with us in our conversations about our own marriage ingredients? We know abiding in you is our most prosperous place of existence. And yet, we don't always prioritize it. We know that in each other, you have placed treasure troves of delights to help sharpen and shape us into the very being you always intended, but we often respond in our flesh rather than with our open spirit. Help us to forgive one another and let it start with ourselves. Thank you for the ultimate sacrifice of your son and for your perfect blood that was poured out for the atonement of our sins. May this practice please you. May it be like a sweet aroma for your throne room as we emulate your love to one another.
May it be the sealed ingredients of steadfast love for our marriage.
And may others bear witness to its divine scent. In your precious name, Jesus, Amen.

"Y" is for Your Time

Individual Pouring In & Pouring Out

Key Scripture: *"Very early in the morning, while it was still dark, Jesus got up, left the house and went off to a solitary place, where he prayed" (Mark 1:35, NIV).*

Healthy marriages require individual growth so that each spouse can pour into the marriage from a place of wholeness. But often, people start here with a focus on themselves and their individual growth rather than on time-in together. This can sometimes create division from the very beginning. Because we have made a sacred commitment to one another, we would like to have a prelude of time-in before time-out in order to build on our relationship and process through any trials that arise. However, we also understand there is a simultaneous need for time-out, as we can't pour from an empty cup. Common self-help rituals aren't the finite solution; instead, from the living waters flow life and renewal.

Discussion & Exercises: Time & Energy Audit: The purpose of this activity is to help you design weekly rhythms that make sense to your family and don't overburden one spouse.

- Consider mind, body, and spirit prioritization of "me" time that leads to "mwe" time (as mentioned in Volley).
- Ideas can include personal therapy; meditation on the Word; prayer time (e.g., women's small groups); physical training/workout time (e.g., adult sports); reading time; sacred space in the home; health routines (e.g., supplements, doctors, sleep); friendship time; and gender-specific events (e.g., women's getaway).

"Y" is for Your Time
Individual Pouring In & Pouring Out

Spiritual Blindspots: This is a critical area of emphasis when it comes to self-help and self-care. We can become focused on our mental, spatial, financial, and physical needs and forget the critical prioritization of spiritual needs. Make sure this is the first focus, not the last.

Personal Rhythms & Replenishment: How does each spouse refuel spiritually, emotionally, and physically?

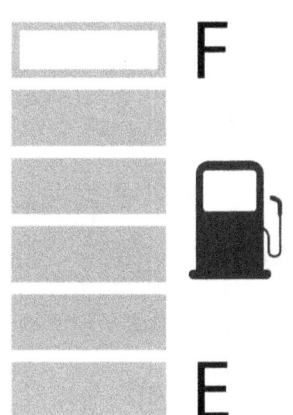

- What does Sabbath look like together?
- How can we support each other's spiritual growth without judgment or condemnation?
- Consider other areas as well, such as chores, expectations, and needs.
- Can you hire outside support to help with cleaning, laundry, or the lawn?
- Understanding each other's expectations can support the designing of a new personal flow, which will lead to a fresh martial flow.

Reevaluating Flow: What shifts can we make to create more balance in our home?

- Consider personal/ marital fasting practices. Could this be implemented monthly /weekly?
- Can we integrate more dedicated time spent with one another throughout the day/week (e.g., wake up earlier for coffee/tea time together or eat together as a family)?

"Y" is for Your Time
continued...

PRAYER COVERING FOR RECIPE

Sweet Jesus, you inspire me through your spiritual practices of solitude: refueling in the Father, meditation, prayer, fasting, and beyond. We thank you for modeling this for us so we don't become prideful or fixed on "me" but rather recenter ourselves on God. We are thankful that you, too, are concerned with our well-being and that we can find the fullness of joy, health, wealth, and fulfillment in you. You lack nothing. We pray you would bountifully bless our time individually so that it may flow into our sacred marriage, which is meant to exude the wonders and miracles of your sacrificial love. We honor you. We magnify you. We thank you. And we love you. In your beautiful name, we pray, Amen.

Acknowledgments

Books like these don't just come to life on a whim. They require attention, massaging, designing, curating, grafting, editing, and marketing. But above all, they require abiding. The concept and timing of this book were God designed. In a time where marriage is mutated rather than celebrated, we are taking a stand for the original intention and the coming union of the Bridegroom and His bride.

To our editor, Sharon Miles Freese, thank you for refining our words with patience and excellence, ensuring that every page speaks truth, clarity, and love into the hearts of readers. Your keen eyes and dedication to detail have been invaluable.

To the design and publishing team, your creativity and skill have been the backbone of development to bring this book to life. From the authors' coordination and implementation to the cover design and final interior layout, your work has beautifully captured the heart of this message.

We want to acknowledge the bravery of the authors and their spouses. These stories aren't easy ones to share, but your time and tears have not been in vain because, as Paul shares in 2 Corinthians 12:19 (NIV), "'My grace is sufficient for you, for my power is made perfect in weakness.' Therefore, I will boast all the more gladly about my weaknesses, so that Christ's power may rest on me." Your strength and courage in enduring will bless generations to come.

And to our family and friends, your unwavering support, patience, and steadfast prayers have been integral assets to our sacrificial love stories of redemption. God's power pouring through you in love and wisdom helped carry us through the storms.

Above all, may God get the glory. Every word, every story, and every lesson within these pages is a testament to His love, grace, and faithfulness. May this book bring healing, restoration, and victory to every marriage it touches.

F.I.T. PRESS

Your story doesn't just matter for you, it matters to move others!

1 CHRONICLES 16:24 (NLT)
*Publish His glorious deeds among the nations.
Tell everyone about the amazing things he does.*

A Christian Publishing House dedicated to turning messages into movements. On mission to mobilize the critical voices for such a time as this. Specializing in co-hort compilations,to make way for writers to collaborate with other prolific members of the Body of Christ. Our works open conversations around mental, physical, relational, financial and spiritual health and wholeness journeys, often directly associated to our rooted identity and purpose driven life.

Learn More & Don't Wait to Get Published!

F.I.T. in FAITH PRESS

"Publish his glorious deeds among the nations.
Tell everyone about the amazing things he does."
1 Chronicles 16:24

As a Christian Publishing House dedicated to bringing the stories of founders, innovators, and trailblazers to life, we invite you to shop from our individual authors, devotionals, and entrepreneur series!

Scan to purchase your copy!

Ladies! Beauty Awaits from the inside-out and outside-in.

We will explore every detail of God's wondrous creation. Starting with YOU! This wellness retreat is an immersive experience intended to get you back to the basics (mind, body, and HOLY spirit) by heightening your senses to what matters most: your vertical alignment, so you can horizontally serve, share, and SHINE!

Fella's! The Great Outdoor Awaits!
Embark. Elevate. Expand. Explore.

Getting primal to perform at our highest potential as men, husbands, fathers, and leaders by activating our sonship. Join us on this "unforget-table, epic, and life changing" adventure that will catalyze you to exist in your power, authority, and passion.

Contact: hello@thefoundercollective.org

founder COLLECTIVE

This is a movement of empowered legacy building, chain breaking, pioneers, liberating others to stand in freedom, firm in their identity, and activating authority as Kingdom citizens. Join the movement today!

JOIN US WEEKLY AT THE TABLE!

let's find out your
PROFIT INDENITY

Reveal Your Passion and Spiritual Gifts Connection to Start & Grow Your Business

TAKE THE QUIZ TODAY!

HAVE YOU EVER WONDERED?

What's my purpose?

How can I use my giftings as a global messenger for God?

How are my spiritual gifts connected to Kingdom wealth?

How does my passion propel my profit?

SUBSCRIBE & LEAVE A REVIEW FOR A SHOUTOUT ON AIR!

The ones on a mission to turn their message into a movement!

This show was designed for Declaring Truth, Transforming Narratives & *Catalyzing Christians to Speak, Write, Build & Testify.*

JOIN THE F.I.T. in Faith Network Resource Hub!

IT'S TIME TO ACTIVATE YOUR *god dream*

DOWNLOAD NOW!

The F.I.T. in Faith Network Resource Hub will serve as a growth tool for you as a Fierce Female ready to Fight The Good Fight.

Speak, Write, Build, Testify

Count this app as your Aaron and Hurr on your fulfilling and sometimes hard days of blazing the trail of your purpose-driven calling.

- SOUND BIBLICAL BUSINESS SUPPORT
- COURSES & CONTENT BUILDING HELP
- TRAINING & IMPLEMENTATION TOOLS
- TEMPLATES & TESTIMONIES
- QUICK START RESOURCES
- FINANCIAL TRAJECTORY PLANS & MODELS

We are a company DEVELOPING & DEPLOYING MESSENGERS *through* publishing, podcasting and platform development!

We help develop, nurture, and grow services, retreats & events for Founders, Innovators, and Trailblazers on a mission to turn their God-given messages into movements for Kingdom expansion!

www.ingramcontent.com/pod-product-compliance
Lightning Source LLC
Chambersburg PA
CBHW081154070526
44583CB00021B/2831